Seneca History written by Dean Six

Published by Page-Frederiksen Publishing Company
Greensboro, NC

Sales Agent: Replacements, Ltd.
Greensboro, NC

Front Cover (From Left):
1934-1 (Sherbet), Cut 800 (Cordial), Stem 155 (cobalt Wine), Cut 800 (Goblet), 926-1 (Juice), 1482-2 (Wine).

Back Cover (From Left):
4816-1 (Plate), Cut 876 (Goblet), Wakefield - Cut 367 (prone Goblet), Cut 726 (Goblet), Cut 1032 (prone Cordial), Windsor - Cut 777 (Footed Tumbler), Cut 859 (Bell).

Additional copies of this book
may be ordered from:

Replacements, Ltd.
1089 Knox Road
PO Box 26029
Greensboro, NC 27420

1-800-562-4462

@ $24.95 per copy.
Add $2.00 postage and handling

Crystal: Cut 907 by Seneca
China: Queen Anne by Syracuse
Flatware: Wedgwood by International Silver Company (Sterling, 1924)

SENECA GLASS COMPANY

1891-1983

A Stemware Identification Guide

Bob Page and Dale Frederiksen

Miscellaneous Decorations

Goblet
993-Dec.501

Sau. Champ
993-D 502

Goblet
9936-GD453

Sau. Champ
9936-GD453

Goblet
152-GD451

Goblet
152-GD449

Goblet
190-GD Lenox

Goblet
9936-GD461

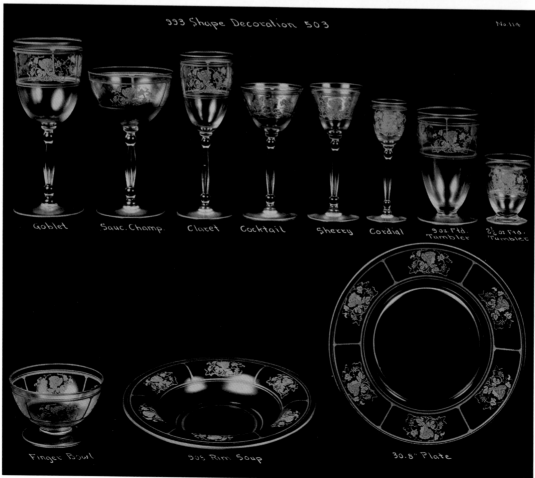

993 Shape Decoration 503

No.114

Goblet   Sauc.Champ.   Claret   Cocktail   Sherry   Cordial   9 oz Ftd. Tumbler   2½ oz Ftd. Tumbler

Finger Bowl   503 Rim Soup   30.8" Plate

IV

CONTENTS

ACKNOWLEDGEMENTS

We would be remiss if we did not acknowledge the many people who have helped us gather the information used in this book. Some have supplied magazine advertisements, others catalogs, and still others actual pieces from the factory. In doing the research, we were able to meet with former factory employees, friends and collectors of Seneca Glass, and others who bought pieces of the glass because they found Seneca to be attractive and tasteful.

Thanks to all who have had a part, however big or small, in helping us compile this book.

Thank you: Mrs. Gordon Rountree, Steven Collins, Beverly Rosenow, Robert Friedrich, Linda Haden, Wayne Fetty, Adriel Cohen, Robert "Tippy" Buck, Katherine Rousseau, Delores Fleming, Tom Rogers, Linda Pellegrin, Anis Catlett, Jerry Gallagher, John Weimer, Theodorine Jacquet Brown (daughter of Seneca Glass blower Leon F. Jacquet), Ogaretta Miller, Raymond Isner, and Drew Kiszka, owner of the Glasshouse Grill located in the old Seneca factory.

A special thanks needs to be said to a group of friends who made it much easier to gather information for this volume. Thank you *Linda and Michael Hall, Jim and Marjie Wylie, and Dean Six* for your efforts in making this book possible!

FOREWORD

This crystal guide was designed to make researching of stemware patterns as easy as possible. Our purpose was to create an informative book on the various patterns (cut, etched, or otherwise decorated) that the Seneca Glass Company produced during its 92 years in existence. We were not looking to attribute values to the various patterns, but to provide a handy guide for identifying patterns. In our effort to get as much information as possible, we used company catalogs, brochures, magazine ads, factory samples, and information from our broad range of customers.

This book is divided into two main sections for research purposes.

The first section shows representations of the various shapes or "blanks" that we have been able to attribute to Seneca Glass Company. When known, the factory numbers are listed. The page numbers shown indicate where patterns appearing on the various stems are pictured in the second section. At the end of this section are two pages of what we call "easily-confused stems" because of their similarity in stem or bowl shape.

In section two, patterns are shown as they would appear on each shape, in stem number order. These patterns were created using computer line drawings. Though we have tried to make each image as accurate as possible, some may be distorted due to the source of the original. With each picture, we have included various descriptive information, such as a cutting or etching number or color. In some instances, the pattern name or number was unknown to us. We have included these pictures also, assigning each a number for reference purposes.

Though we have worked months gathering information, there are still many patterns listed in company price lists that we have not been able to identify. These patterns are listed following each stem that the pattern would appear on. Any assistance in identifying these would be greatly appreciated!

We hope that this reference guide provides help in identifying Seneca crystal for years to come.

SENECA GLASS COMPANY

For almost a century, Seneca Glass of Morgantown, West Virginia was a premier producer of fine lead glass in colors, crystal, and with elegant cuttings and numerous decorative treatments.

Opening in Seneca County, Ohio in 1891, the company was composed primarily of immigrant glassworkers who had been neighbors in the Black Forest region of Germany. They relocated to Fostoria, Ohio where they opened shop in the then-vacated plant of the Fostoria Glass Company. Although located in an Ohio plant, the newly formed company preferred a West Virginia charter which was granted on December 4, 1891. In 1896 Seneca relocated to Morgantown, West Virginia to take advantage of newly discovered natural gas, available river and railroad transportation, and local offers of land. The same German families retained significant control of the factory and its management until the very last few years of the company's long history. Initial growth was impressive: by 1897, 250 glass workers were employed at Seneca.

Early production included hand-blown fine lead crystal in a variety of forms: tumblers, bar bottles, covered candy jars, decanters, finger bowls, sugars and creamers, nappies, water sets, vases, and endless stemware. While this book deals primarily with Seneca stemware, remember that many patterns offered countless additional pieces. One of Seneca's significant lines at the turn-of-the century was thin, blown, etched tumblers for bars and advertising tools, from whiskey to banks. The thin glass tumblers were the disposable paper cup of their day and thousands and thousands were required. A fire destroyed the factory in June of 1902; however, the furnace with 14 pots remained and shortly thereafter a rebuilding program had the company back in production.

Glass blower Leon Jacquet is readily supplied by 'gatherer' Raymond Isner.

Designs can be found on Seneca glass using nearly every technique known to the glass artist. Sand blasted, acid etched, plate etched, needle etched, hand cut, and others were produced in the decorating rooms of Seneca. Rich cut glass from Seneca was so complex as to have required twelve hours to cut a single object. In addition, diversity was a key to survival for Seneca. In the 1920's the factory inventories included extensive crackle ware production. A 1931 list shows opal (milk) glass being available and a 1971 list included thousands of dollars of the Krinkle pattern for Carbone, a special order customer. Colored glass appeared in the 1920's and would remain at varying levels due to consumer demands until the factory's close.

▲ Artwork of Seneca's first location, the Fostoria Glass Factory in Fostoria, Ohio, taken from an early 1900's Seneca catalog.

◀ Aerial photograph of Seneca's main plant c. 1956 located in Morgantown, West Virginia. Its accessibility by railway and river made this an ideal location. (WEST VIRGINIA AND REGIONAL HISTORY COLLECTION, WEST VIRGINIA UNIVERSITY LIBRARIES)

Morgantown has been home to several dozen glass houses, Seneca being the first. Over the years the company maintained a national and international reputation for quality wares. From providing endless elegant sets for American Embassies the world over to special commissions for then Vice-President Lyndon Johnson (the Johnson's chose the Epicure pattern for their private use) or for the President of Liberia, Seneca has been held in the highest regard. The marketplace for Seneca was usually high-end because of the time and workmanship involved in finishing some of its wares. Unlike others in the cut crystal industry, Seneca could fill orders for patterns purchased decades earlier. The fact that they were the producers of the glass blank and the cutters gave them access to molds unused for years, and their archives allowed pattern comparison for matching a goblet from years before.

In 1924, when colored and elegant glass was stylish and in vogue, Seneca employed 159 men and 57 women. Women at that time worked primarily in the decoration departments. Through the years, the numbers of employees varied as did the production levels. By 1911 Seneca production required a second plant to be opened. This was built in Star City, West Virginia, about two miles from

Shown in shop #15 is glass blower Leon Jacquet (on platform) supported by 'gatherer' Raymond Isner, 'carry-in boy' Ogaretta Miller, and 'finisher' Mr. Ludwig. It was common for several family members to work in the same factory. Leon and Ogaretta were siblings whose father also worked at Seneca Glass as a cutter.

Seneca's first plant, and employed an additional 63 men and 7 women. Production at the second factory was largely tumblers and undecorated ware. The second factory operated into the 1930's. Depression era production included not only colorless glass but also cobalt, and the "up-to-date transparent colors" as a 1932 advertisement termed their light green, topaz, and other "depression era" colors.

Specialty cutting and decorating was an important part of the Seneca business. The Seneca glass sold through the famous store of John Wanamaker in Philadelphia for the executive mansion of Liberia consisted of 218 dozen in a special design with crests cut in each item. Other well known Seneca customers included the Ritz Carlton Hotel, Boston; Pinnacle Club, New York; Tudor Room of the Sheraton Palace Hotel, San Francisco; Marshall Field and Company, Chicago; B. Altman Company, New York; Tiffany's, New York; Richs, Atlanta and Neiman-Marcus, Dallas. Seneca glass was well represented in many elegant settings.

The colors produced over the years were many and in the 1970's would include Accent Red (ruby and crystal combinations), Amber, Buttercup (yellow), Cinnamon (brown), Delphine Blue (a light blue), Ritz Blue (cobalt), Sahara (a light amber), Gray (a smoky color), Moss Green (a dark earthy green), Lime Green, Peacock Blue, Black and Plum (amethyst). In these later years most of these colors were used in accent pieces such as covered candy bowls, vases, stacking Christmas tree containers, and pattern molded stemware (not including the cut glass lines).

With elegant tables popular for brides in the 1940's Seneca experienced a return to prosperity and colorless cut wares became the predominate line. As early as 1953 Seneca foresaw the fading interest in elegant table settings and started producing their Driftwood pattern. This mouth blown, hand crafted line remained in production almost 30 years, making it Seneca's most recognizable production item. Driftwood was originally introduced for "informal dining" in four shapes: iced tea, highball, water tumbler, and juice, and in four colors: Honey, Bottle Green, Amethyst

Smoke and Clearwater Crystal. Driftwood would grow over the years to include offerings in plates, pitchers, covered candy dishes, vases and nearly a dozen beverage glasses in a multitude of colors.

The 1970's saw other "informal" patterns offered trying to capture the shift from formal elegant glassware. Many patterns were very short-lived, perhaps one or two years. Then in 1982, Seneca Glass Company was sold to a group of investors from Malaysia. The new owners organized the company under the name of Seneca Crystal Incorporated. By August of 1983 the firm had filed for bankruptcy and the inventory and equipment sold at public auction. Company archives included hundreds of factory samples of glass cut over the preceding decades, many with detailed notations of cut, shape and for whom they were made. A very small portion of Seneca archival material is preserved at West Virginia University, in the regional history collection. The Seneca machinery and molds went to diverse new owners. Some of the one-of-a-kind, 80-year old goblets had their feet broken off and the stems polished to be converted to bells. Few of the stemware molds have been re-issued since the closing of Seneca and then in extremely limited production. Some items such as the two sizes of ginger jars were re-issued in cobalt and nicely hand cut, but in a manner unlike that of Seneca. All re-issues have been in soda lime and not lead glass. Due to practical limitations there is little likelihood that Seneca molds will see additional use.

Today the Seneca Glass Company building remains. Portions of it have been carefully adapted to house a complex of retail stores and a restaurant decorated with a glass house theme in the commons areas.

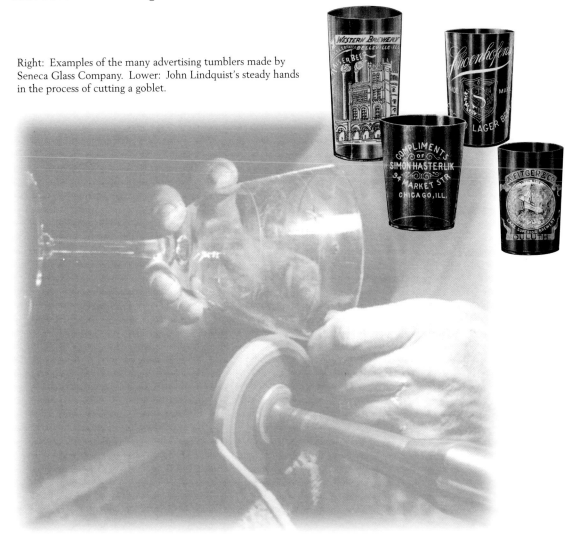

Right: Examples of the many advertising tumblers made by Seneca Glass Company. Lower: John Lindquist's steady hands in the process of cutting a goblet.

CATALOG PHOTOGRAPHY

Shown in the next few pages are selected examples of items as they were shown in company catalogs. Each item was clearly photographed to enhance sales of each item. In Seneca's later years, patterns that did not have immediate success in sales would be removed from the catalog and any further advertisements. Also shown in this section are the various stems of the Frank Schoonmaker Gourmet Wine series, a line of wine glasses made to accompany the 1235 Epicure line.

Line No 916 - Cutting 870

1

Goblet

Saucer Champagne

Claret

Sherbet

Cocktail

Wine

No 30 - 8 inch Salad Plate

Footed Finger Bowl or Low Fruit

Cordial

No 8101 10 oz Full Sham Tumbler

6 oz Footed Tumbler

9 oz Footed Tumbler

12 oz Footed Tumbler

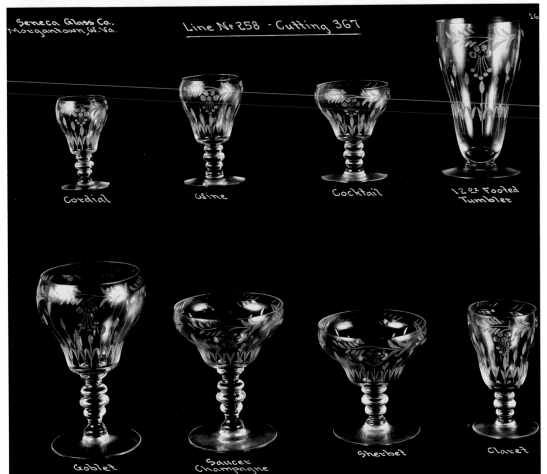

Line No 258 - Cutting 367

16

Cordial

Wine

Cocktail

12 oz Footed Tumbler

Goblet

Saucer Champagne

Sherbet

Claret

Goblet

Saucer
Champagne

Sherbet

Cocktail

Wine

Footed Finger Bowl
or Low Fruit

Sherry

Cordial

Claret

Parfait

12 oz Footed
Tumbler

No 260. Bar Bottle
Cut 859

870z - 10 oz
F/s Tumbler
Cut 859

No 85 - 7½ oz
O.F. Cocktail
Cut 859

220 - 2½ oz
Sham
Whiskey
Cut 859

No 90. 26 oz
C/n & Flute
Bar Bottle
Cut 900.

812 n - 2½ oz
Sham Whiskey
Cut 367

9450 - 10 oz
Sham Toddy
Cut 367

870z - 12 oz
Tumbler
Cut 367

No 90. 26 oz
C/n & Flute
Bar Bottle
Cut 367

870z - 10 oz F/s Tumb
Cut 900

85 - 7½ oz O.F. Cocktail
Cut 900

220 - 2½ oz
Sham Whiskey
Cut 900

XIV

Seneca Glass Co.,
Morgantown, W. Va.

No. 1. 12"
Cake Salver

No. 7. 9 inch
Salad Bowl
Cutting 841

No. 7. 12 inch
Salad Bowl
Cutting 849

No. 7. 14" Tray. Cutting 841
Also made in 11 and 12 inch.

No. 7. 7 inch
Salad Bowl
Cutting 900

No. 4 - 16 inch
Centerpiece
Cutting 806

Punch Bowl & Ladle
Cutting 326

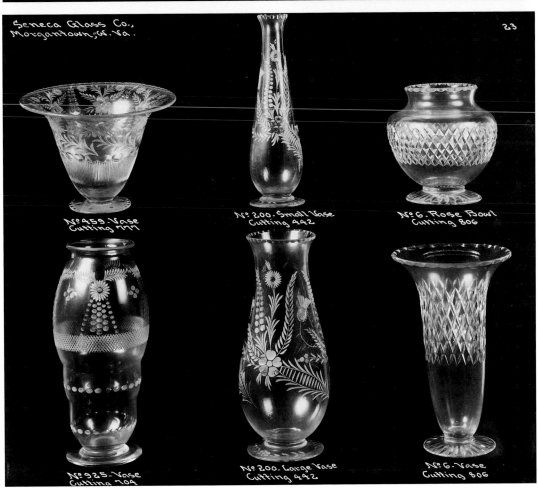

Seneca Glass Co.,
Morgantown, W. Va.

No. 459. Vase
Cutting 747

No. 200. Small Vase
Cutting 442

No. 6. Rose Bowl
Cutting 806

No. 925. Vase
Cutting 704

No. 200. Large Vase
Cutting 442

No. 6. Vase
Cutting 806

Seneca Glass Co.,
Morgantown, W. Va.

24

No 4. Oil
Cut 568

No 7. Oil
Cut 692

No 1. Oil
Cut 428

No 8. Oil
Cut 636

No 5. Oil
Cut 532

No 2. 2 Pt.
Decanter
Cut 791.

A 899
Wine
Cut 791.

No 3. 2 Pt.
Decanter
Cut 880

925
Wine
Cut 880.

No 1. 2 Pt.
Decanter
Cut 859

908
Wine
Cut 859

No 5. 1 Pt.
Decanter
Cut 859

Seneca Glass Co.
Morgantown, W. Va.

26

No 485 - 6 inch
Compote
Cutting 367

Covered
Mustard
Cutting 778

Covered
Marmalade
Cutting 778.

No 102 - 7 inch
Compote
(Also made in 8 inch)
Cutting 556

No 499 7 inch
Compote
Cutting 597

1 Lb. Covered
Candy Jar
Cutting 778

No 6 - 7 inch
Compote
Cutting 889

XVI

No 16
Sugar & Cream
Cut 718

No 6
Sugar & Cream
Cut Beaded Edge

No 2. Dinner Bell
Cut 789

No 1934
Sugar & Cream
Cutting 717

No 1. Dinner Bell
Cutting 590

No 1 - 6"
3 Toed Nappy
Cutting 806

No 1 - 6"
Handled Nappy
Cutting 859

2 Handled
Cream Soup
Cutting 374

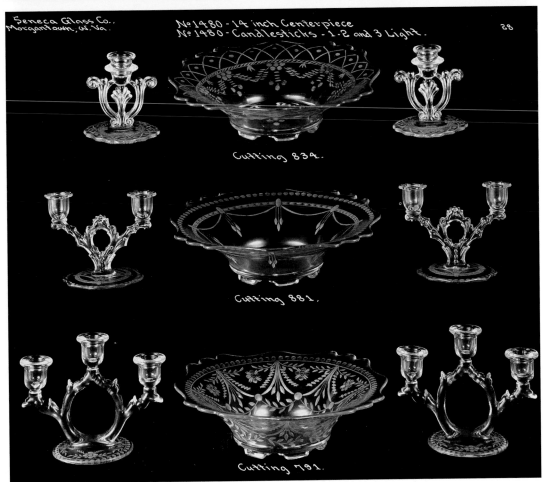

No 1480 - 14 inch Centerpiece
No 1480 - Candlesticks - 1-2 and 3 Light.

Cutting 834.

Cutting 881.

Cutting 791.

XVII

A Complete Liquor Service - Cutting 900

Seneca Glass Co.,
Morgantown, W. Va. 29

No 12. 3½ oz
Cocktail.

No 220. 2½ oz
Sham Whiskey

No 85. 7½ oz
Old Fashioned
Cocktail

No 905½. 4 oz
Whiskey Sour

No 3. Ice Tub

No 9491.
14 oz
Tumbler

Bitters Bottle
and Tube.

No 8701. 10 oz
Full Sham
Tumbler

No 7. 14 inch
Serving Tray.

No 90. 26 oz Bar Bottle
Cut Neck & Flutes.

No 10. 54 oz Jug.

Line No 476 - Cutting 900

Seneca Glass Co.
Morgantown, W. Va.
6

Goblet

Saucer
Champagne

Hock

Rhine Wine

Claret

Hot Whiskey

Cocktail

Creme De
Menthe

Sherry

Cordial

12 oz
Footed
Tumbler

9 oz
Footed
Tumbler

6 oz
Footed
Tumbler

4 oz
Footed
Tumbler

30 - 8 inch
Plate

Footed
Finger Bowl

Hollow Stem
Saucer
Champagne

Hollow Stem
Champagne

Sherbet

Wine

Parfait

Line 1934 - Cut 777.

Seneca Glass Co.,
Morgantown, W. Va.
4

Goblet

Saucer Champagne.

Sherbet

Claret.

Wine.

No. 30 - 8 inch Salad Plate.

Finger Bowl

Cordial

Cocktail

12 oz. Ftd. Tumbler

Line 1940 - Cutting 799

Seneca Glass Co.,
Morgantown, W. Va.
5

Goblet

Saucer Champagne.

Claret

Cocktail

Cordial

Claret 1939/C798.

Goblet 920/C862

Goblet 1937/C43

Goblet 1937/C794.

Goblet 1937/C939

Goblet 1938/C795

XIX

Line No 1936 - Cut 779

Seneca Glass Co.
Morgantown, W. Va.

3

Goblet

Saucer Champagne

Claret

Wine

Cocktail

No 30 - 8 inch Salad Plate.

Finger Bowl

Cordial

Sherbet

12 oz Ftd. Tumbler.

Line 3050 - Cutting 935

Seneca Glass Co.,
Morgantown, W. Va.

9

Goblet

Saucer Champagne.

Claret

Wine

Cordial

908 - 6½" Baked Apple.

908 - 9" Rim Soup.

Goblet
Gut 627

Goblet
C 636

Goblet
C 651

Goblet
C 671

Goblet
C 705

Goblet
C 706

Goblet
C 846

Goblet
C 847

Goblet
C 848

Goblet
C 967

Goblet
C 1073

Goblet
C 1074

Goblet
492/M603

Sherbet
492/M603

Goblet
9936/M1028

Goblet
476/M1026

9 oz Ftd.
Tumbler
1282/M819

Dutch Brandy
17/M 1028

Goblet
912/M1025

Goblet
1482/C1033

Goblet
1482/C442

Goblet
1482/C583

Goblet
1482/C987

Goblet
1482/C619

Goblet C1012

Goblet C1013

Goblet C1014

Goblet C1015

Goblet C1016

Goblet C1021

Sau. Champ. C1021

No. 1 Bell C590

No. 2 Bell C771

No. 3 Bell C121

No. 3 Bell C660

No. 3 Bell C1013

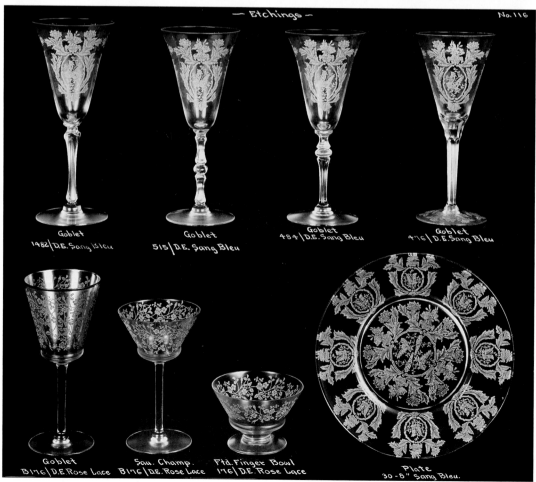

Goblet 1482/D.E. Sang Bleu

Goblet 515/D.E. Sang Bleu

Goblet 484/D.E. Sang Bleu

Goblet 476/D.E. Sang Bleu

Goblet B176/D.E. Rose Lace

Sau. Champ. B176/D.E. Rose Lace

Ftd. Finger Bowl 176/D.E. Rose Lace

Plate 30-8" Sang Bleu.

Goblet
518-C1046

Goblet
518-C1064

Goblet
518-C1076

Goblet
518-C1077

Goblet
616-C1078

Goblet
616-C1079

Goblet
926-C1075

Seneca Glass Co.,
Morgantown, W. Va.

25

Cutting 900
No. 4-14 inch Console Bowl
Also made in 12 inch

No. 30 Rolled Edge Candlestick

Cutting 889
No. 6-14 inch Console Bowl
Also made in 12 inch

No. 4-8 inch Candlestick
Also made in 10 and 12 inch.

Cutting 853
No. 4-14 inch Heavy Footed Bowl
Also made in 12 inch.
No. 4-10 inch Candlestick
Also made in 8 and 10 inch.

Champagne Tulip

Johannisberg

Frank Schoonmaker®
Gourmet Wine Glasses

#1 CHAMPAGNE TULIP
8 1/2", 8 oz.

#2 JOHANNISBERG
6 1/8", 6 oz.

#3 MAGNUM
5 7/8", 10 oz.

#4 VIN DU PAYS
5 3/8", 8 oz.

#5 CABERNET
6 1/2", 9 oz.

#6 SOLERA
5 1/8", 5 oz.

#7 V. S.O.P.
4 1/2", 7 oz.

#8 CHATEAU
6", 7 oz.

Magnum

Vin Du Pays

Cabernet

V.S.O.P.

Chateau

Solera

SENECA GLASS COMPANY

Stems By Shape and Number

9
Page 13

10
Page 13

12
Page 13

14
Page 13

15
Page 13

16
Page 13

17
Page 13

19
Page 13

20
Page 13

25
Page 13

26
Page 13

26
Page 13

26
Page 14

27
Page 14

30
Page 14

31
Page 14

33
Page 14

34
Page 14

34
Page 15

35
Page 15

36
Page 15

37
Page 15

38
Page 15

40
Page 15

41
Page 15

45
Page 15

51
Page 15

56
Page 16

60
Page 16

61
Page 16

65
Page 16

70
Page 16

77
Page 16

77 t/s
Page 16

80
Page 16

81
Page 17

82
Page 17

83
Page 17

84
Page 17

85
Page 17

87
Page 17

88
Page 17

89
Page 17

90
Page 17

91
Page 17

92
Page 17

93
Page 17

94
Page 17

95
Page 17

100
Page 17

100 1/2
Page 18

101
Page 18

128
Page 18

150
Page 18

3

152
Page 19

155
Page 19

156
Page 19

160
Page 19

164
Page 20

170
Page 20

176
Page 21

180
Page 21

180 1/2
Page 22

190
Page 22

190 opt
Page 22

200
Page 24

207
Page 24

210
Page 24

211
Page 24

212
Page 24

213
Page 24

215
Page 24

252
Page 25

256
Page 25

256 t/s
Page 25

258
Page 25

258
Page 25

259
Page 25

260
Page 26

263
Page 26

290
Page 26

295
Page 26

297
Page 26

298
Page 26

299
Page 27

300
Page 27

301
Page 27

307
Page 27

307
Page 27

310
Page 28

325
Page 28

331
Page 28

349
Page 28

350
Page 28

352
Page 28

355
Page 29

358
Page 30

360
Page 30

361
Page 30

388
Page 30

388
Page 30

393
Page 31

400
Page 32

404/7112
Page 32

405
Page 32

405
Page 32

450
Page 32

452
Page 32

4

459
Page 32

460
Page 33

465
Page 33

466
Page 33

470
Page 33

472
Page 33

475
Page 33

476
Page 34

477
Page 37

479
Page 37

481
Page 37

482
Page 37

483
Page 38

484
Page 39

485
Page 39

486
Page 40

488
Page 40

492
Page 40

493
Page 41

496
Page 42

496
Page 42

498
Page 42

499
Page 42

506 t/s
Page 43

508
Page 43

515
Page 43

516
Page 44

517
Page 44

518
Page 44

520
Page 45

526
Page 46

528
Page 46

532
Page 46

553
Page 47

578
Page 48

616
Page 48

641
Page 48

700
Page 48

708
Page 49

748
Page 49

857
Page 49

903
Page 49

905
Page 50

905 1/2
Page 51

907
Page 51

908
Page 52

909
Page 53

910
Page 54

912
Page 54

913
Page 55

914
Page 55

915
Page 56

916
Page 56

917
Page 57

5

918
Page 57

922
Page 57

923
Page 58

925
Page 58

926
Page 58

957
Page 58

959
Page 59

960
Page 59

966
Page 60

970
Page 60

970
Page 60

971
Page 60

972
Page 60

974
Page 61

975
Page 61

976
Page 61

978
Page 61

981
Page 61

982
Page 62

993
Page 62

1012
Page 63

1025
Page 63

1030
Page 63

1034
Page 63

1050
Page 63

1055
Page 63

1060
Page 63

1072
Page 63

1107
Page 63

1108
Page 63

1200
Page 63

1201
Page 64

1202
Page 64

1203
Page 64

1204
Page 65

1205
Page 65

1207
Page 65

1208
Page 65

1210
Page 65

1213
Page 65

1214
Page 65

1217
Page 65

1219
Page 66

1220
Page 66

1235
Page 66

1258
Page 66

1258 1/2
Page 66

1282 t/s
Page 67

1282
Page 67

1293
Page 68

1350
Page 68

1400
Page 69

1476
Page 69

1479
Page 69

1482
Page 70

1488
Page 71

1556
Page 71

1599
Page 71

1605
Page 71

1693
Page 72

1726
Page 72

1780
Page 72

1820
Page 72

1892
Page 72

1933
Page 72

1934
Page 73

1936
Page 73

1937
Page 73

1938
Page 73

1939
Page 74

1940
Page 74

1941
Page 74

1951
Page 74

1952
Page 75

1962
Page 75

1963
Page 75

1964
Page 76

1965
Page 77

1966
Page 78

1967
Page 79

1969
Page 79

1970
Page 80

1971
Page 80

1972
Page 80

1973
Page 80

1974
Page 81

1975
Page 81

1976
Page 81

1977
Page 81

1978
Page 81

1980
Page 82

1985
Page 82

2000
Page 82

2257
Page 82

2258
Page 82

2493
Page 82

2502
Page 82

2503
Page 83

2672
Page 83

2690
Page 83

2812
Page 83

3000 t/s
Page 83

3050
Page 83

3050
Page 84

3214
Page 84

3600
Page 85

3635
Page 85

3691
Page 85

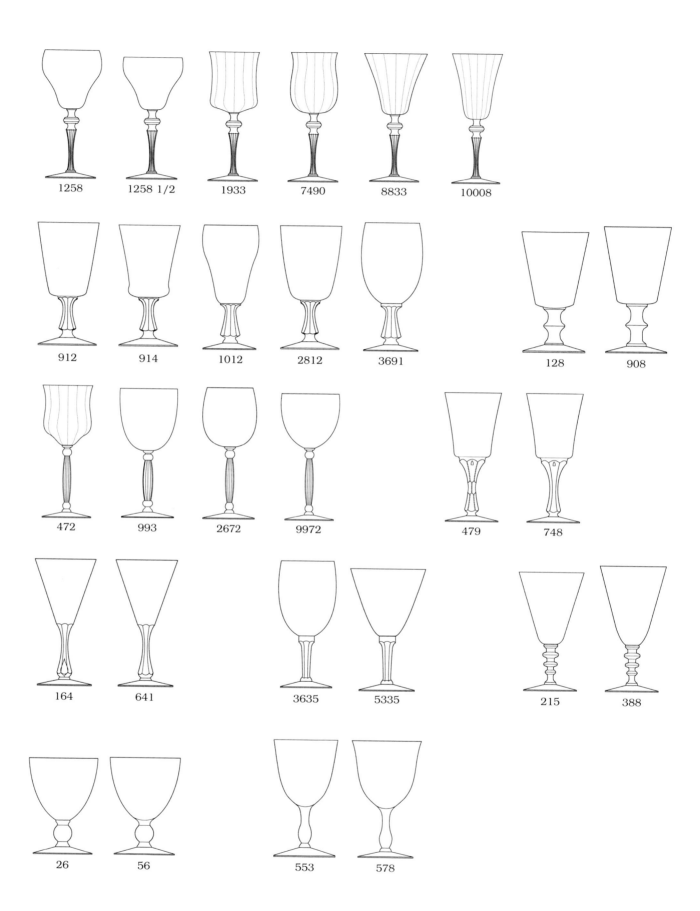

1258   1258 1/2   1933   7490   8833   10008

912   914   1012   2812   3691   128   908

472   993   2672   9972   479   748

164   641   3635   5335   215   388

26   56   553   578

SENECA GLASS COMPANY

Stems By Pattern and Number

Stem 9

Stem 10

Stem 12

Stem 14

Stem 15

Stem 16

Stem 17

Stem 19

Engraved 283
19

NE 16
19

Stem 20

Stem 25

Stem 26
"Heritage"
Crystal or Charcoal Bowl

Stem 26
Cut Ball

Bedford
Cut 1115
26

Other Stem 26 Patterns:

Cut 1107   Cut 1280
Cut 1113   Cut 1282 "Flight"
Cut 1189   Cut 1298
Cut 1279

Duchess
Cut
26

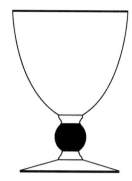

Gold Ball
Gold Trim on Rim and Foot
26

26-1
Cut
26

Stem 26

Stem 27

Stem 30

Stem 31

Stem 33

Stem 34

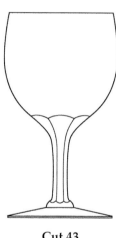

Cut 43
34

Cut 263
34

Cut 560
34

Cut 653
34

Cut 4390
34

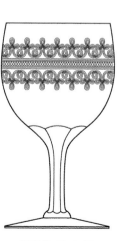

NE 8, Cut 43
34

NE 23, Cut 43
34

Stem 34

Stem 35

Stem 36

Stem 37

Stem 38

Stem 40

Stem 41

Stem 45

Stem 51

Starlite
Cut 1214
51

51-1
Cut
51

51-2
Cut
51

51-3
Cut
51

Other Stem 51 Patterns:
Cut 1208 "Desert Bloom"
Cut 1218 "Ming"
Cut 1287 "Evening Star"

15

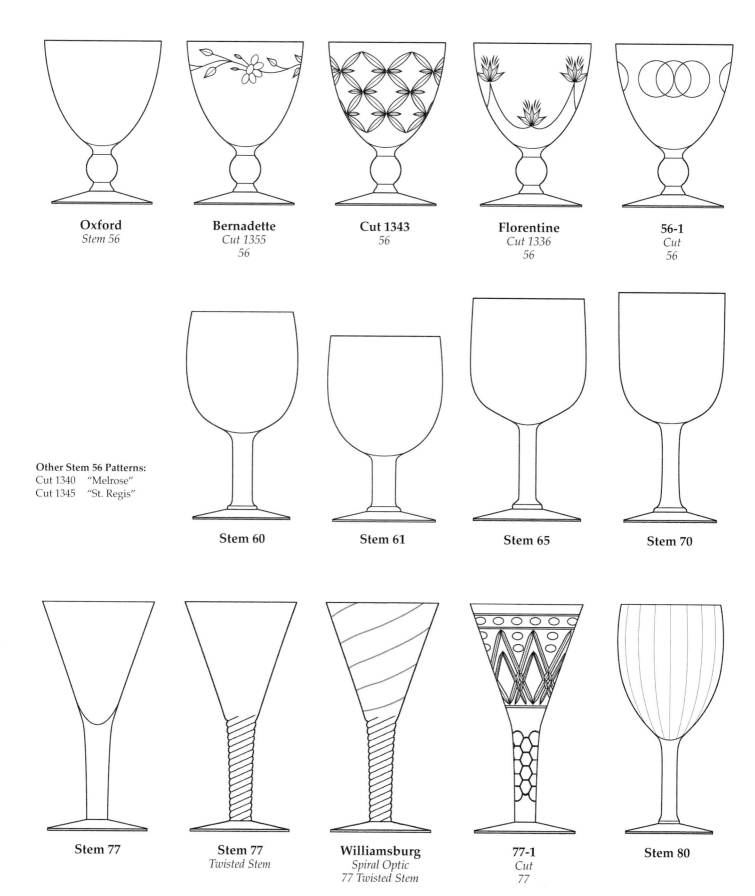

Oxford
Stem 56

Bernadette
Cut 1355
56

Cut 1343
56

Florentine
Cut 1336
56

56-1
Cut
56

Other Stem 56 Patterns:
Cut 1340   "Melrose"
Cut 1345   "St. Regis"

Stem 60

Stem 61

Stem 65

Stem 70

Stem 77

Stem 77
Twisted Stem

Williamsburg
Spiral Optic
77 Twisted Stem

77-1
Cut
77

Stem 80

Stem 81   Stem 82   Stem 83   Stem 84   Stem 85

Stem 87   Stem 88   Stem 89   Stem 90   Stem 91

Stem 92   Stem 93   Stem 94   Stem 95   Stem 100

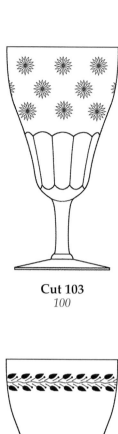

Cut 103
100

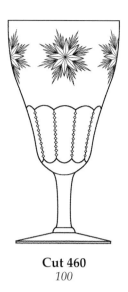

Cut 460
100

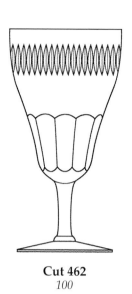

Cut 462
100

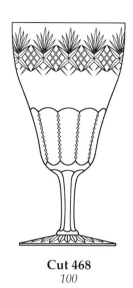

Cut 468
100

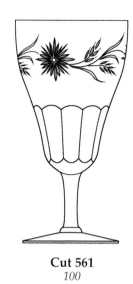

Cut 561
100

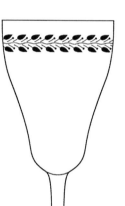

Engraved 1
100

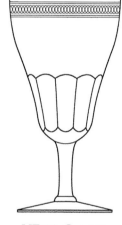

NE 14, Cut 463
100

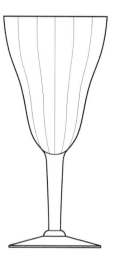

Stem 100 1/2

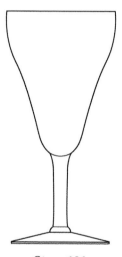

Stem 101

Stem 128

Bradford
Cut 1276
128

Dundee
Cut 1275
128

Martha Washington
Cut 1274
128

Other Stem 128 Patterns:
Cut 1273 "Lorelei"
Cut 1277 "Karen"
Cut 1332

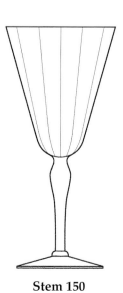

Stem 150

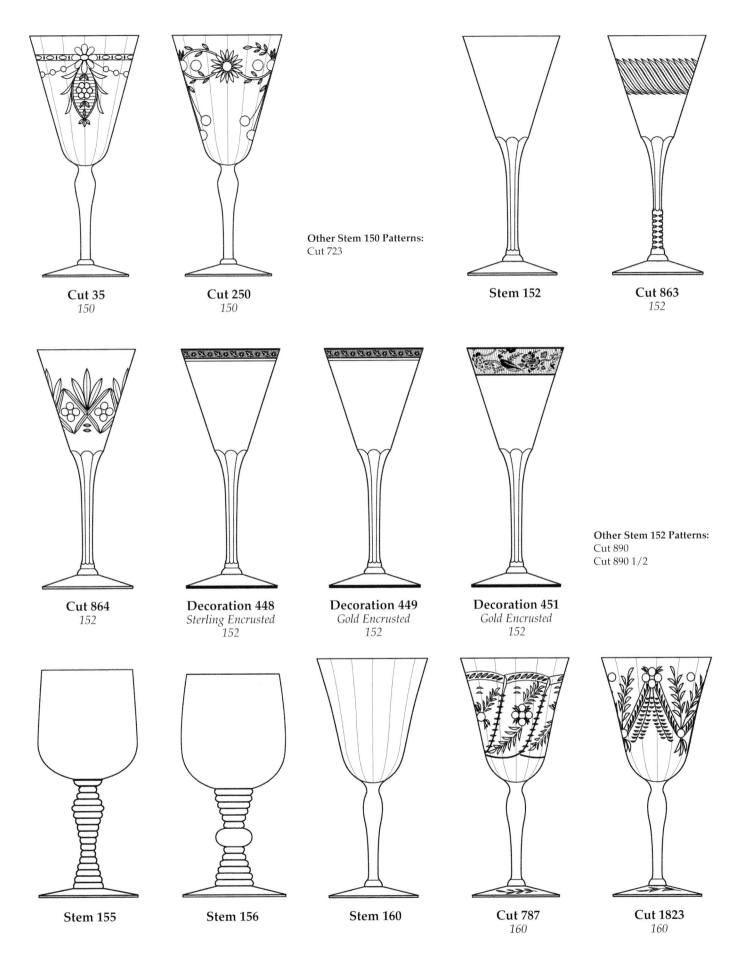

Cut 35
150

Cut 250
150

Other Stem 150 Patterns:
Cut 723

Stem 152

Cut 863
152

Cut 864
152

Decoration 448
Sterling Encrusted
152

Decoration 449
Gold Encrusted
152

Decoration 451
Gold Encrusted
152

Other Stem 152 Patterns:
Cut 890
Cut 890 1/2

Stem 155

Stem 156

Stem 160

Cut 787
160

Cut 1823
160

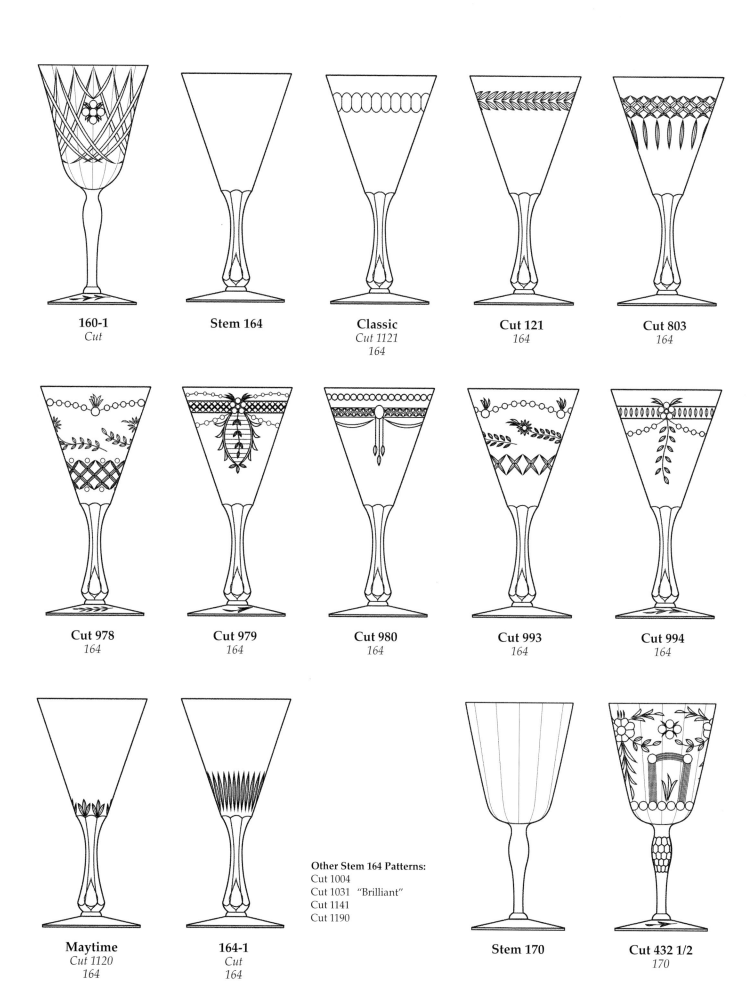

160-1
Cut

Stem 164

Classic
Cut 1121
164

Cut 121
164

Cut 803
164

Cut 978
164

Cut 979
164

Cut 980
164

Cut 993
164

Cut 994
164

Maytime
Cut 1120
164

164-1
Cut
164

Other Stem 164 Patterns:
Cut 1004
Cut 1031 "Brilliant"
Cut 1141
Cut 1190

Stem 170

Cut 432 1/2
170

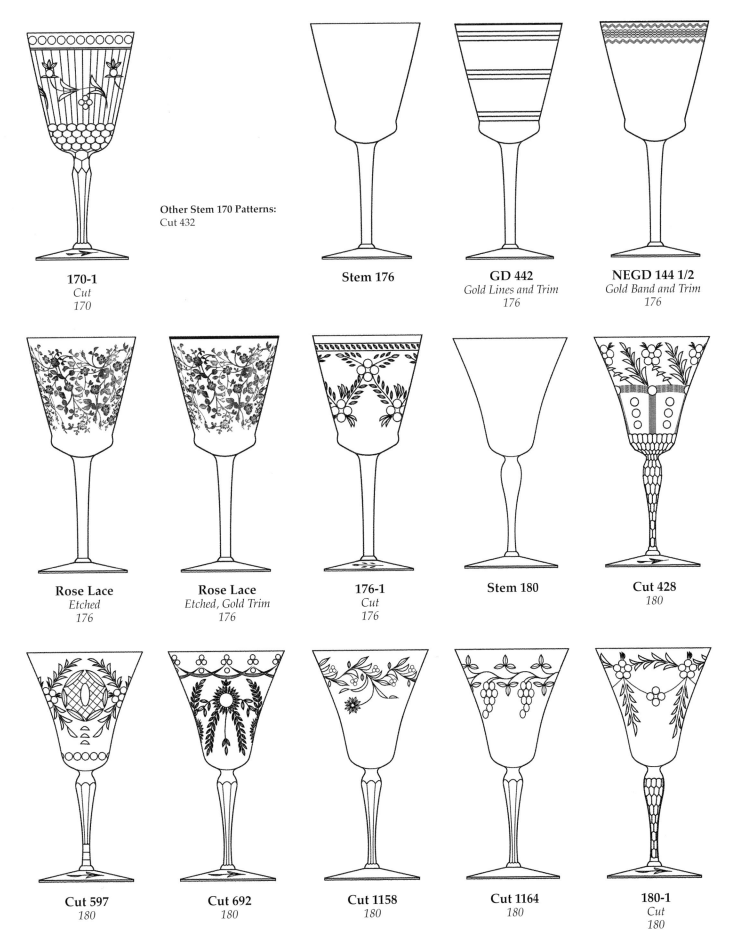

170-1
Cut
170

Other Stem 170 Patterns:
Cut 432

Stem 176

GD 442
Gold Lines and Trim
176

NEGD 144 1/2
Gold Band and Trim
176

Rose Lace
Etched
176

Rose Lace
Etched, Gold Trim
176

176-1
Cut
176

Stem 180

Cut 428
180

Cut 597
180

Cut 692
180

Cut 1158
180

Cut 1164
180

180-1
Cut
180

21

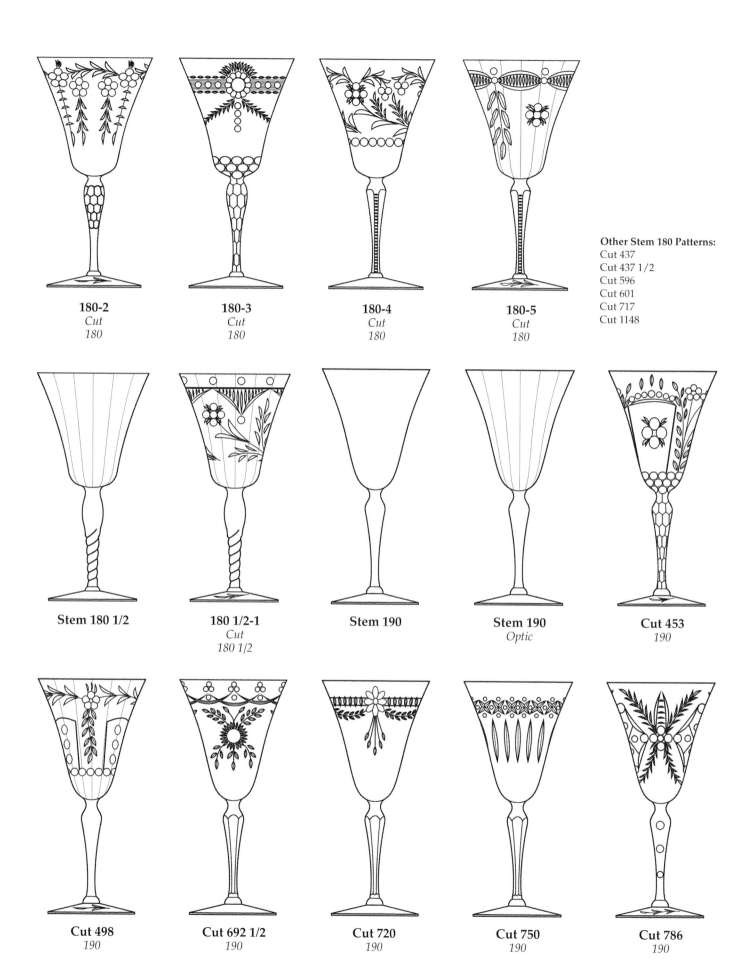

180-2
Cut
180

180-3
Cut
180

180-4
Cut
180

180-5
Cut
180

Other Stem 180 Patterns:
Cut 437
Cut 437 1/2
Cut 596
Cut 601
Cut 717
Cut 1148

Stem 180 1/2

180 1/2-1
Cut
180 1/2

Stem 190

Stem 190
Optic

Cut 453
190

Cut 498
190

Cut 692 1/2
190

Cut 720
190

Cut 750
190

Cut 786
190

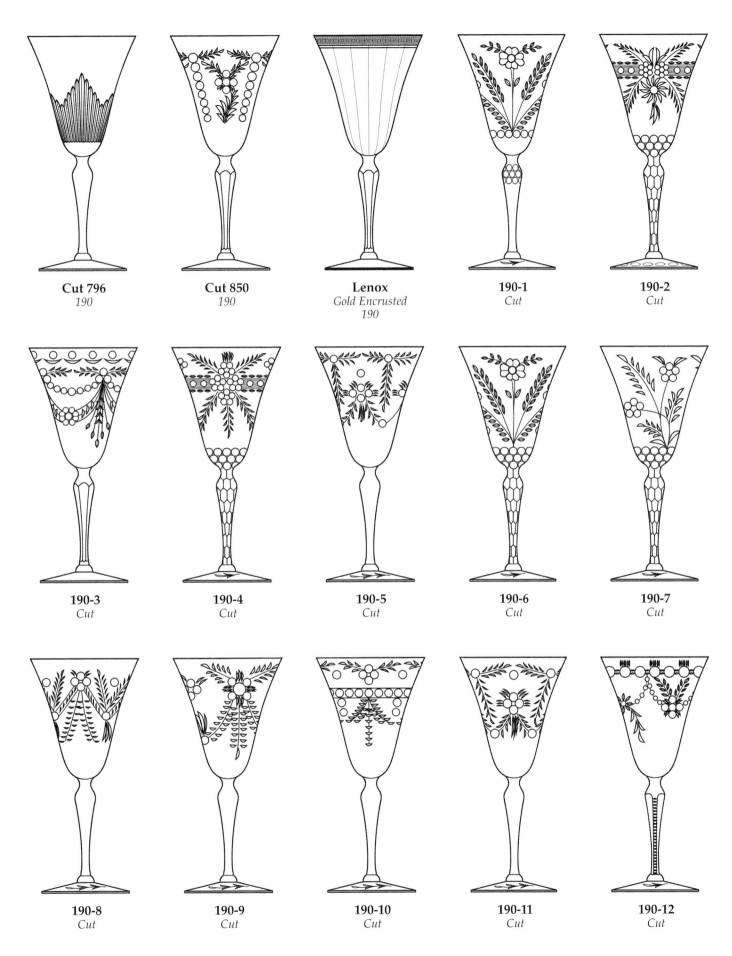

Cut 796
190

Cut 850
190

Lenox
Gold Encrusted
190

190-1
Cut

190-2
Cut

190-3
Cut

190-4
Cut

190-5
Cut

190-6
Cut

190-7
Cut

190-8
Cut

190-9
Cut

190-10
Cut

190-11
Cut

190-12
Cut

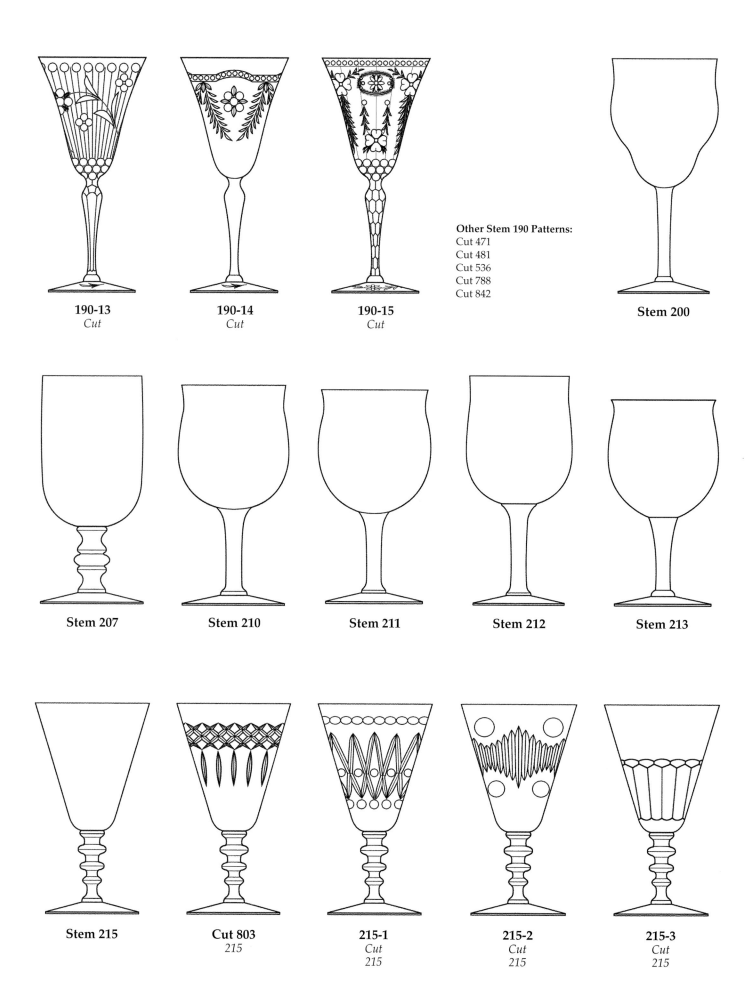

190-13
Cut

190-14
Cut

190-15
Cut

Other Stem 190 Patterns:
Cut 471
Cut 481
Cut 536
Cut 788
Cut 842

Stem 200

Stem 207

Stem 210

Stem 211

Stem 212

Stem 213

Stem 215

Cut 803
215

215-1
Cut
215

215-2
Cut
215

215-3
Cut
215

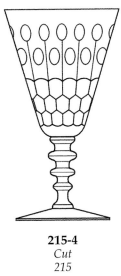

Other Stem 215 Patterns:
Cut 1237
Cut 1239

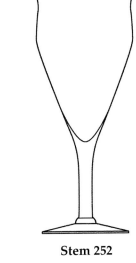

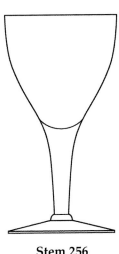

215-4
Cut
215

215-5
Cut
215

Stem 252

Stem 256

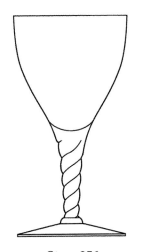

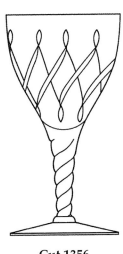

Stem 256
Twisted Stem

Cut 1342
256

Cut 1356
256

Cut 1357
256

Stem 258

Stem 258
Tall Stem

Cut 358
258

258-1
Cut
258

Stem 259
Square Base

Wakefield
Cut 367
259

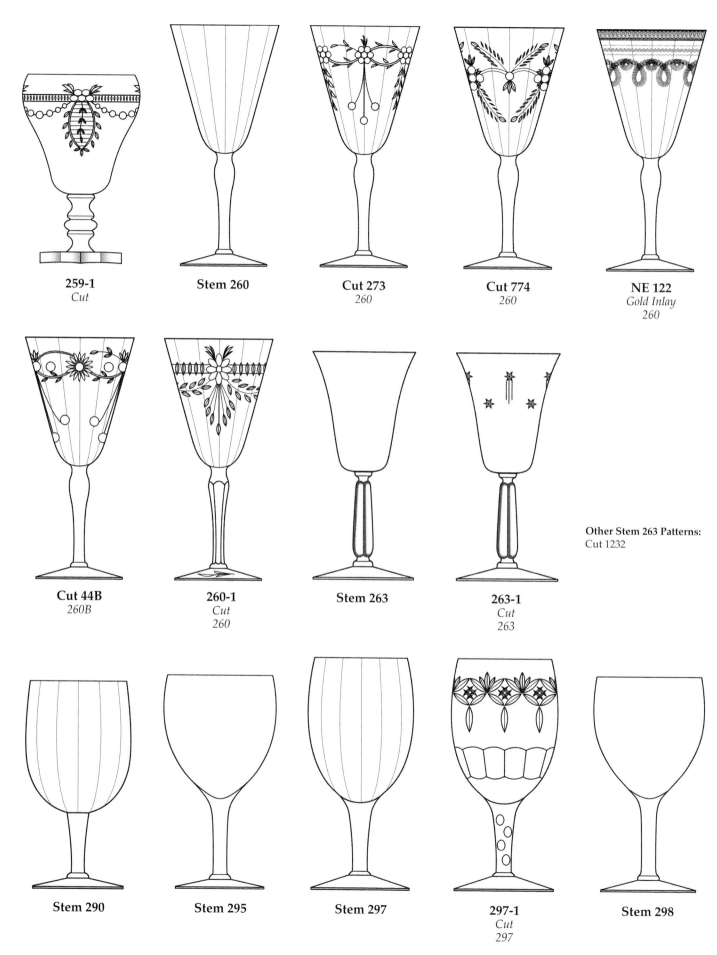

259-1
Cut

Stem 260

Cut 273
260

Cut 774
260

NE 122
Gold Inlay
260

Cut 44B
260B

260-1
Cut
260

Stem 263

263-1
Cut
263

Other Stem 263 Patterns:
Cut 1232

Stem 290

Stem 295

Stem 297

297-1
Cut
297

Stem 298

Stem 299

Stem 300

Engraved 5
300

Engraved 116
300

Grape
Etch 608
300

Pansy
Etch 610
300

300-1
Cut
300

300-2
Cut, Gray Flower
300

Stem 301

Other Stem 301 Patterns:
Cut 360

Pirouette
Stem 307
Clear

Stem 307 was made avail-
able in Ocean Blue, Moss
Green, and Amber, but the
colored stems were not
named.

Arcadia
Cut 1213
307

Gotham
Cut 43
307

307-1
Swirl Optic, Cut 43
307

27

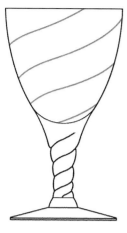

307-2
Swirl Optic, Twisted Stem
307

Other Stem 307 Patterns:
Cut 1310
Cut 1324
Cut 1331
Cut 1335 "Bancroft"
Cut 1354 "Seneca Twist"

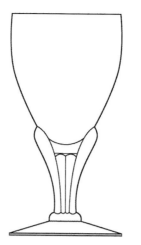

Stem 310
Various Colored Stems

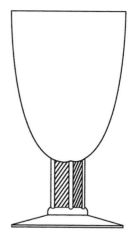

Stem 325
Various Colored Stems

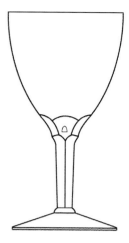

Corinthian
Cut 1300
331

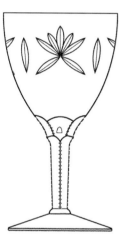

Starflower
Cut 1269
331

Other Stem 331 Patterns:
Cut 1270 "Madison"
Cut 1271
Cut 1272 "Coronet"
Cut 1301
Cut 1302 "West Wind"

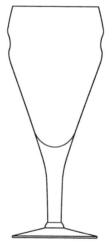

Stem 349

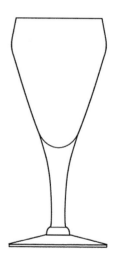

Stem 350

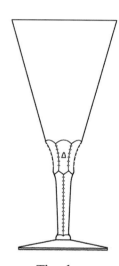

Timeless
Cut 1380
Stem 352

Ardis
Cut 1262
352

Caprice
Cut 1229
352

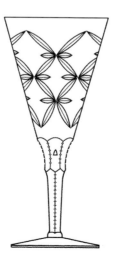

Coronation
Cut 1254
352

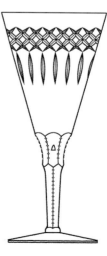

Cut 803
352

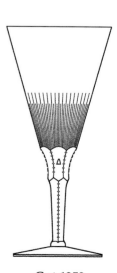

Cut 1252
352

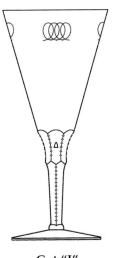

Cut 1330 1/2
352

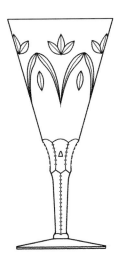

Cut "J"
352

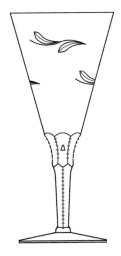

Fleur de Lis
Cut 1227
352

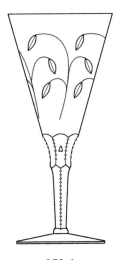

Westwind
Cut 1263
352

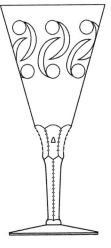

352-1
Cut
352

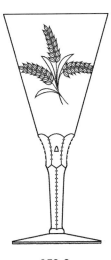

352-2
Cut
352

Other Stem 352 Patterns:
Cut 1230 "Marlboro"
Cut 1231
Cut 1345 1/2

Flair
Stem 355
Crystal

Stem 355 was made available in Peacock Blue, Heather, and Amber. The colored stems are called "Silhouette".

Baronet
Cut 1334
355

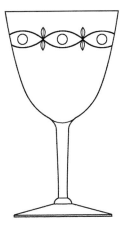

Bellaire
Cut 1319
355

Celeste
Cut 1318
355

Coventry
Cut 1325
355

Cut 1375
355

Garland
Cut
355

Romance
Cut 1337
355

Silver Leaf
Cut 1320
355

Wedding Band
Platinum Band
355

Willow Wind
Cut 1351
355

355-2
Cut
355

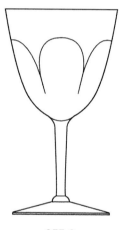

355-3
Cut
355

355-4
Cut
355

355-5
Cut
355

Other Stem 355 Patterns:
Cut 1317 "Lorraine"
Cut 1338 "Garland"
Cut 1346 "Spring Song"
Cut 1358 "Concerto"
Cut 1360 "Tiara"
Cut 1363 "Allure"
Cut 1366 "Meadow Breeze"
Cut 1369 "Minuet"
Cut 1385 "Garland"
Cut 1388 "Vintage"
Cut 1389 "Rose Buds"
Cut 1398

Stem 358

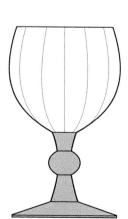

Stem 358
Black Stem and Foot

Cosmopolitan
Cut 43
Stem 360

Stem 361

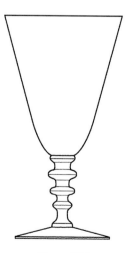

Stem 388

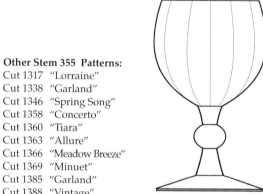

Stem 388
Cut Stem

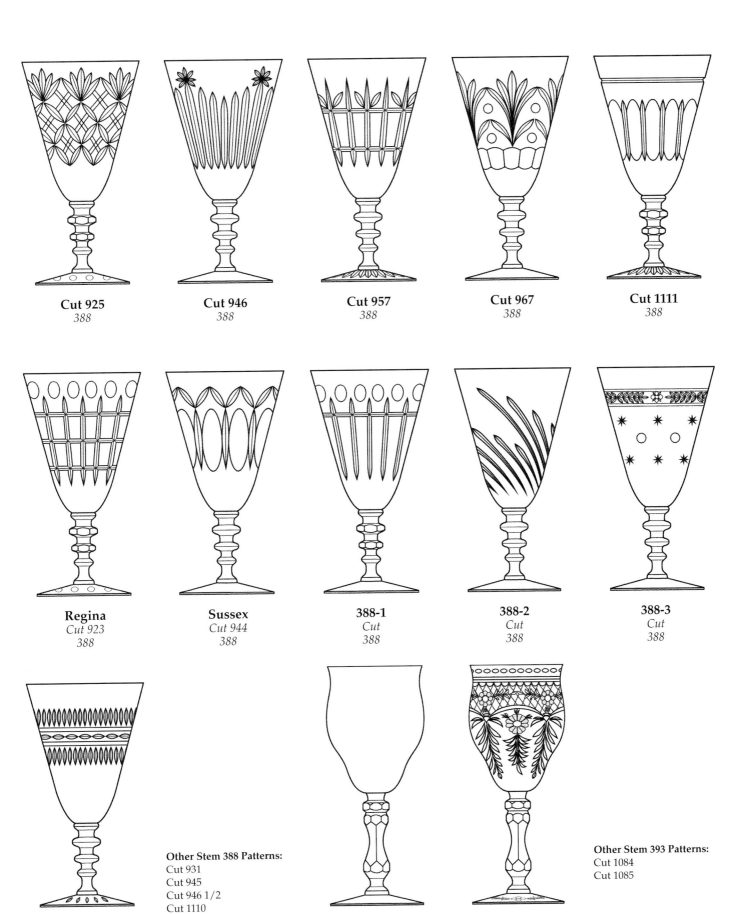

Cut 925
388

Cut 946
388

Cut 957
388

Cut 967
388

Cut 1111
388

Regina
Cut 923
388

Sussex
Cut 944
388

388-1
Cut
388

388-2
Cut
388

388-3
Cut
388

388-4
Cut
388

Other Stem 388 Patterns:
Cut 931
Cut 945
Cut 946 1/2
Cut 1110

Stem 393

393-1
Cut
393

Other Stem 393 Patterns:
Cut 1084
Cut 1085

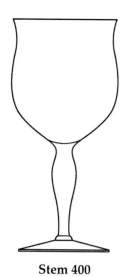

Stem 400

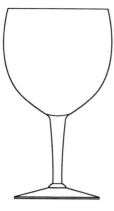

Stem 404
Same as Stem 7112

Connoisseur
Stem 405
Short

Connoisseur
Stem 405
Tall

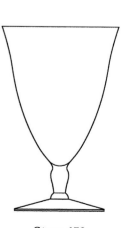

Ballet
Cut 1049
405

Capistrano
Cut
405

Gossamer
Cut 1297
405

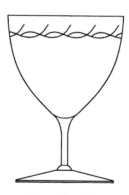

Pine Needles
Cut 1221
405

Sonata
Cut 1326
405

Windfall
Cut 1220
405

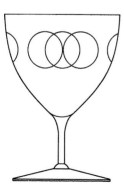

405-1
Cut
405

Other Stem 405 Patterns:
Cut 1282

Stem 450

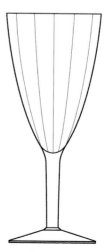

Stem 452

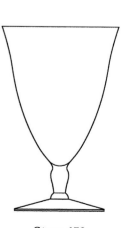

Stem 459

32

Cut 204
459

Stem 460

NEGD 145
Needle Etched, Gold Inlay
460

Stem 465

Cut 33
465

Stem 466
Various Colors

Stem 470

Cut 868
470

Stem 472

Stem 475

Stem 475

Butterfly
Cut 786
475

Cut 31
475

Cut 258
475

Cut 441
475

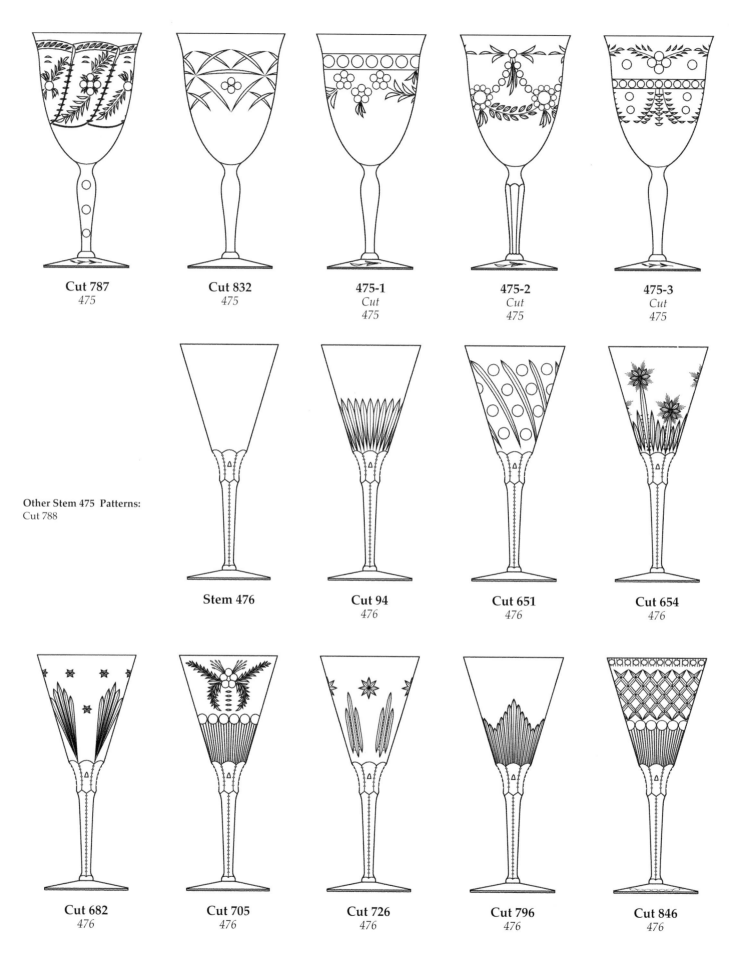

Cut 787
475

Cut 832
475

475-1
Cut
475

475-2
Cut
475

475-3
Cut
475

Other Stem 475 Patterns:
Cut 788

Stem 476

Cut 94
476

Cut 651
476

Cut 654
476

Cut 682
476

Cut 705
476

Cut 726
476

Cut 796
476

Cut 846
476

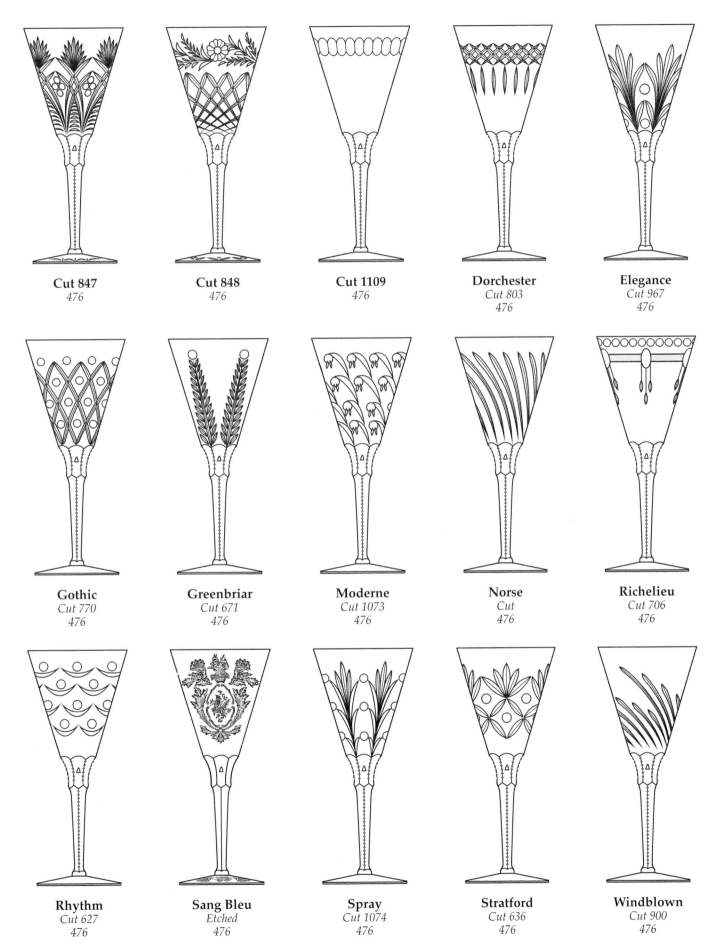

Cut 847
476

Cut 848
476

Cut 1109
476

Dorchester
Cut 803
476

Elegance
Cut 967
476

Gothic
Cut 770
476

Greenbriar
Cut 671
476

Moderne
Cut 1073
476

Norse
Cut
476

Richelieu
Cut 706
476

Rhythm
Cut 627
476

Sang Bleu
Etched
476

Spray
Cut 1074
476

Stratford
Cut 636
476

Windblown
Cut 900
476

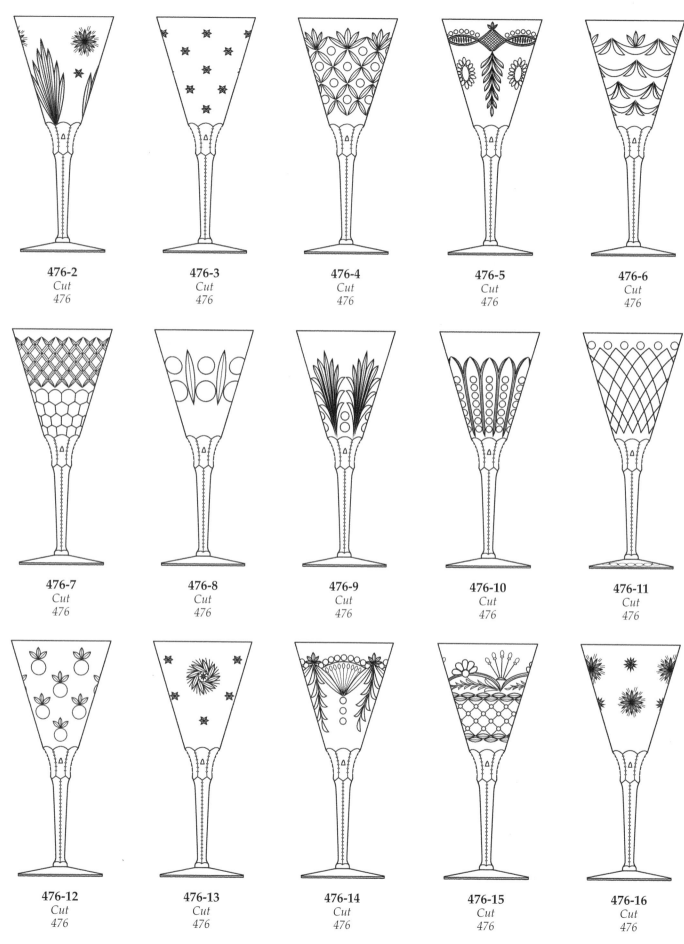

476-2
Cut
476

476-3
Cut
476

476-4
Cut
476

476-5
Cut
476

476-6
Cut
476

476-7
Cut
476

476-8
Cut
476

476-9
Cut
476

476-10
Cut
476

476-11
Cut
476

476-12
Cut
476

476-13
Cut
476

476-14
Cut
476

476-15
Cut
476

476-16
Cut
476

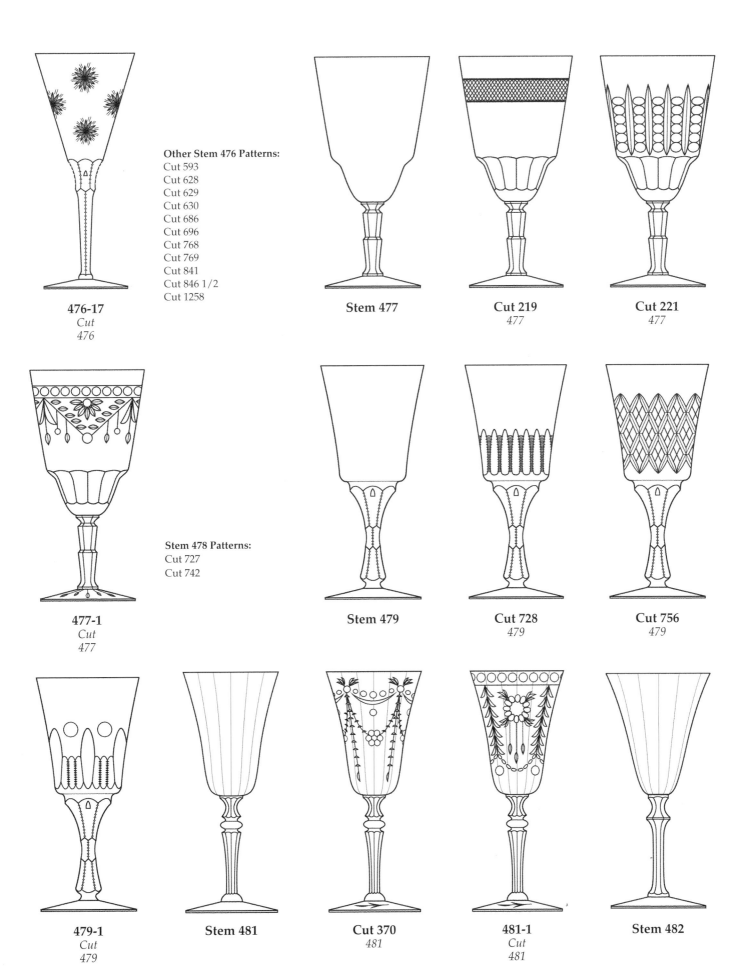

476-17
Cut
476

Other Stem 476 Patterns:
Cut 593
Cut 628
Cut 629
Cut 630
Cut 686
Cut 696
Cut 768
Cut 769
Cut 841
Cut 846 1/2
Cut 1258

Stem 477

Cut 219
477

Cut 221
477

477-1
Cut
477

Stem 478 Patterns:
Cut 727
Cut 742

Stem 479

Cut 728
479

Cut 756
479

479-1
Cut
479

Stem 481

Cut 370
481

481-1
Cut
481

Stem 482

Cut 57
482

Cut 58
482

Cut 61
482

Cut 64
482

Cut 218
482

Cut 259
482

Cut 260
482

Cut 761
482

Cut 1288
482

482-1
Cut
482

Stem 483

483-1
Cut
483

483-2
Cut
483

Other Stem 483 Patterns:
Cut 736

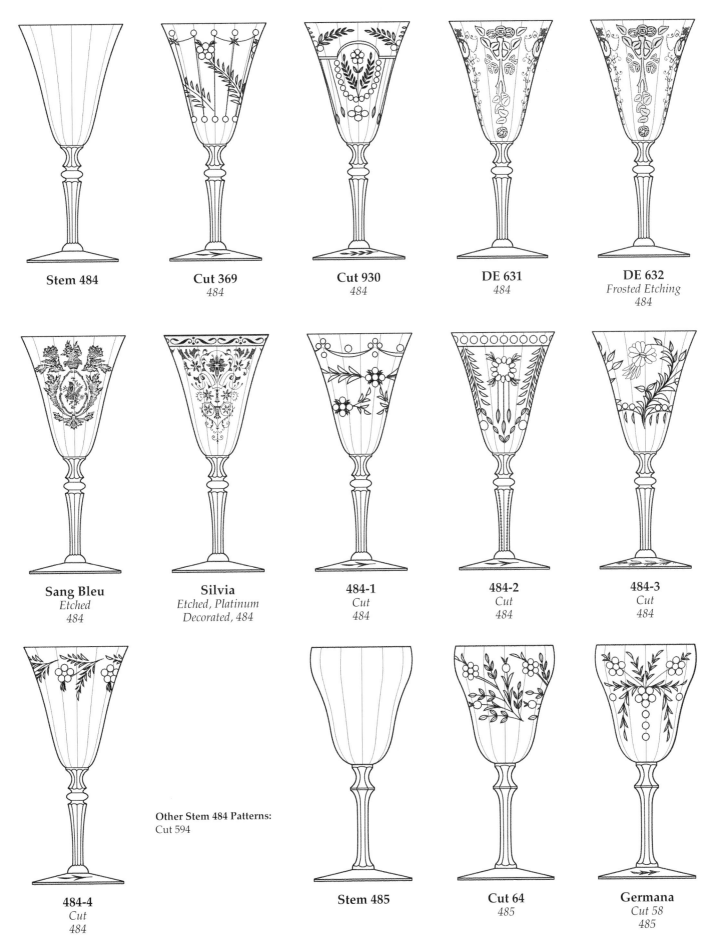

Stem 484

Cut 369
484

Cut 930
484

DE 631
484

DE 632
Frosted Etching
484

Sang Bleu
Etched
484

Silvia
Etched, Platinum
Decorated, 484

484-1
Cut
484

484-2
Cut
484

484-3
Cut
484

484-4
Cut
484

Other Stem 484 Patterns:
Cut 594

Stem 485

Cut 64
485

Germana
Cut 58
485

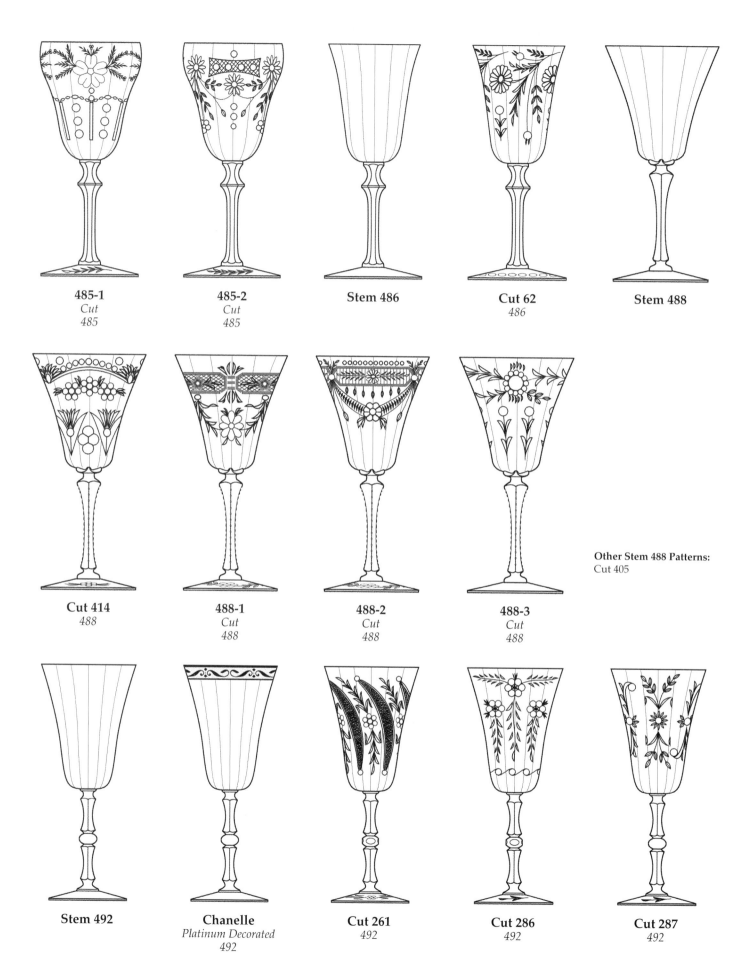

485-1
Cut
485

485-2
Cut
485

Stem 486

Cut 62
486

Stem 488

Cut 414
488

488-1
Cut
488

488-2
Cut
488

488-3
Cut
488

Other Stem 488 Patterns:
Cut 405

Stem 492

Chanelle
Platinum Decorated
492

Cut 261
492

Cut 286
492

Cut 287
492

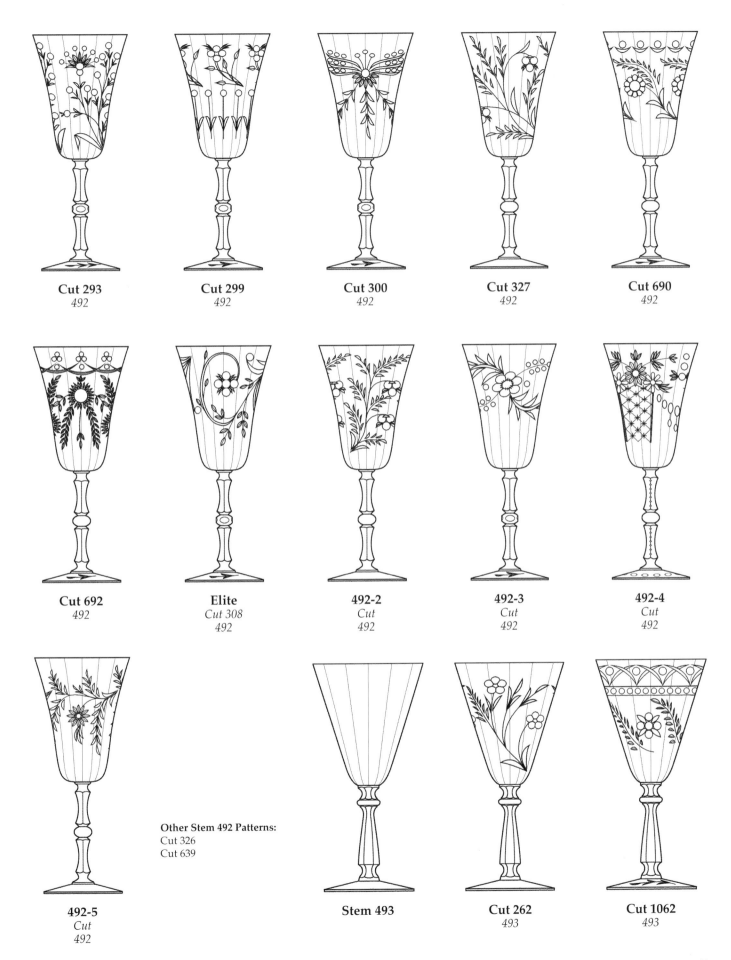

Cut 293
492

Cut 299
492

Cut 300
492

Cut 327
492

Cut 690
492

Cut 692
492

Elite
Cut 308
492

492-2
Cut
492

492-3
Cut
492

492-4
Cut
492

492-5
Cut
492

Other Stem 492 Patterns:
Cut 326
Cut 639

Stem 493

Cut 262
493

Cut 1062
493

41

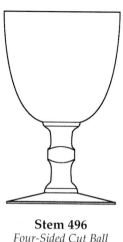

Stem 496
Four-Sided Cut Ball

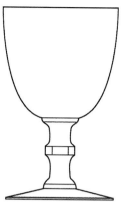

Stem 496
Six-Sided Cut Ball

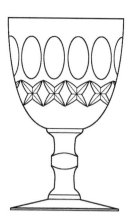

Duchess
Cut 1127
496

Old English
Cut 1128
496

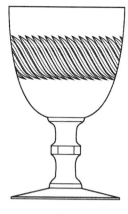

496-1
Cut
496

Stem 498

Stem 499

Cut 367
499

Cut 371
499

Cut 372
499

Cut 373
499

Estes
Etched, Platinum
Decorated, 499

DE 633
499

DE 634
Frosted Etching
499

499-1
Cut
499

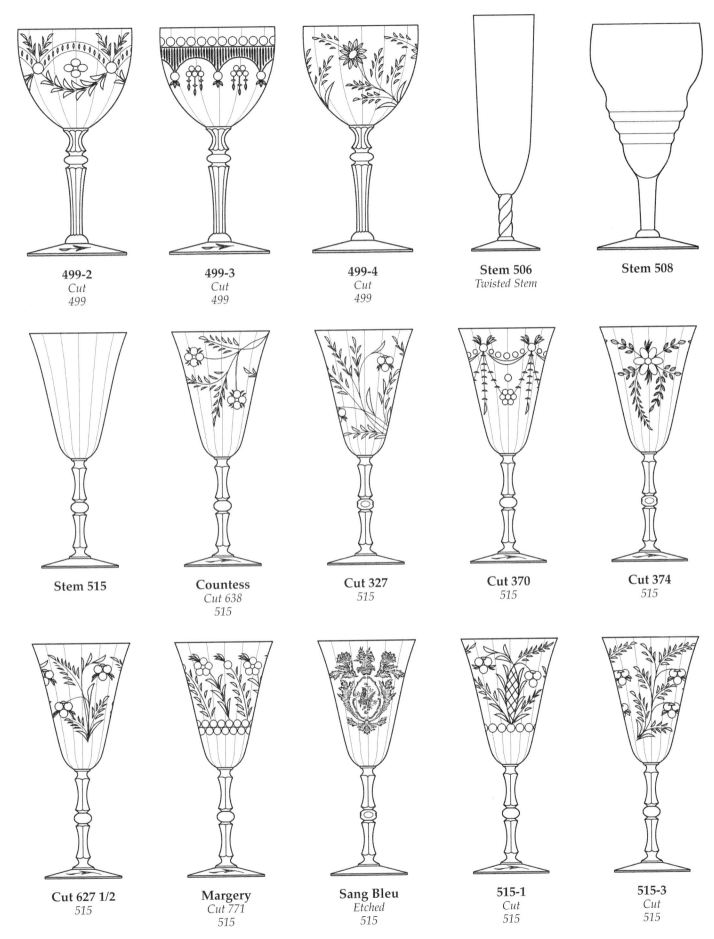

499-2
Cut
499

499-3
Cut
499

499-4
Cut
499

Stem 506
Twisted Stem

Stem 508

Stem 515

Countess
Cut 638
515

Cut 327
515

Cut 370
515

Cut 374
515

Cut 627 1/2
515

Margery
Cut 771
515

Sang Bleu
Etched
515

515-1
Cut
515

515-3
Cut
515

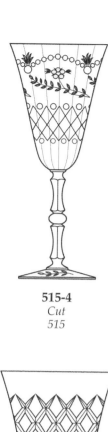

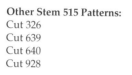

515-4
Cut
515

Other Stem 515 Patterns:
Cut 326
Cut 639
Cut 640
Cut 928

Stem 516
Square Base

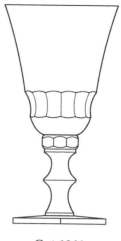

Cut 1041
516

516-1
Cut
516

516-2
Cut
516

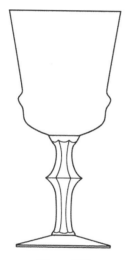

Stem 517

Buttercup
Cut 1162
517

Cut 1046
517

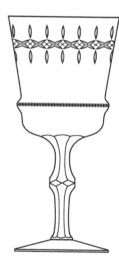

Portland
Cut 1045
517

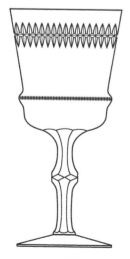

517-1
Cut
517

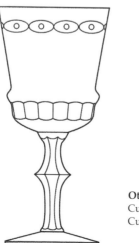

517-2
Cut
517

Other Stem 517 Patterns:
Cut 121
Cut 1104

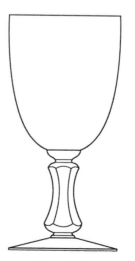

Stem 518

Cut 1046
518

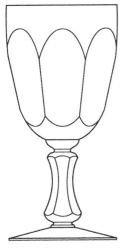

Cut 1047
518

Cut 1055
518

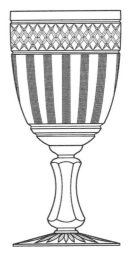

Cut 1064
518

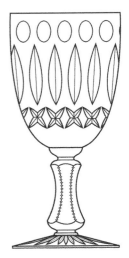

Cut 1077
518

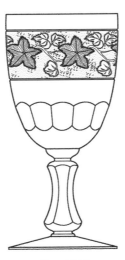

Georgian
Cut 1076
518

Strathmore
Cut 1112
518

Ingrid
Stem 520
Crystal

Stem 520 was made available in Ocean Blue, or was made Charcoal with a crystal stem, but were not named patterns.

Blue Ridge
Cut 1158
520

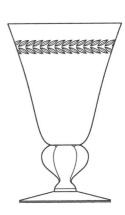

Cut 121
520

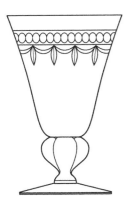

Cut 1134
520

Cut 1164
520

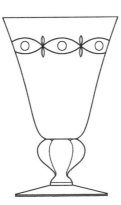

Provincial
Cut 1117
520

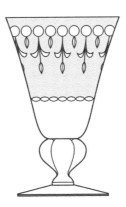

520-1
Cut, Ruby Flashed
520

520-3
Cut
520

520-4
Cut
520

Other Stem 520 Patterns:
Cut 1119 "North Star"

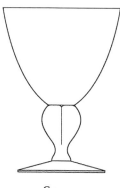

Savoy
Stem 526

Stem 526 was made available with a Moss Green Bowl, an Amber Bowl, and with Gold or Platinum bands, none of which were named patterns.

Charcoal
Gray Bowl
526

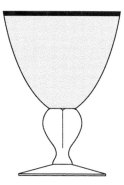

Charcoal Band
Gray Bowl, Platinum
526

Cut 1213
Charcoal Bowl
526

Sahara
Cut 1219
526

Wheat
Cut 1224
526

Stem 528

Stem 532

Billingsley Rose
Cut 1386
532

Cut 1377
532

Fernleigh
Cut 1256
532

Festival
Cut 1251
532

Harvest
Cut 1259
532

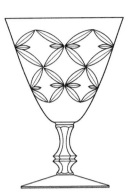

Touraine
Cut 1255
532

Woodcliff
Cut 1347
532

532-1
Cut
532

532-2
Cut
532

Other Stem 532 Patterns:
Cut 1296 "Fleurette"
Cut 1348 "Starfire"
Cut 1376

Stem 553

Stem 553 was made available in Peacock Blue, Heather, and Amber. The colored stems are called "Trousseau".

Stem 553 was also made with a 1/16" platinum band, but was not given a special name.

Astral
Cut 1362
553

Fantasia
Cut 1365
553

Flame
Cut 1381
553

Stellar
Cut 1374
553

553-1
Cut
553

553-2
Cut
553

Other Stem 553 Patterns:
Cut 1368 "Encore"
Cut 1371 "Wildwood"
Cut 1373 "Scandia"

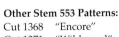

Stem 578

Stem 578 was made available in Peacock Blue, Heather, and Amber. The colored stems are called "Debutante".

Avena
Cut 1372
578

Cut 1379
578

Cynthia
Cut 1361
578

Woodstock
Cut 1370
578

578-1
Cut
578

Other Stem 578 Patterns:
Cut 1359   "Twilight"
Cut 1364   "Corsage"
Cut 1367   "Waverly"
Cut 1377   "Asteric"
Cut 1378

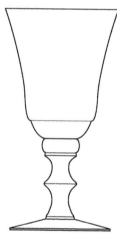

Stem 616

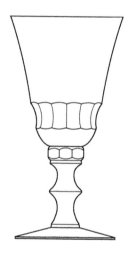

Cut 1041
616

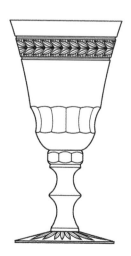

Cut 1078
616

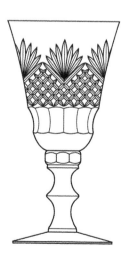

Cut 1079
616

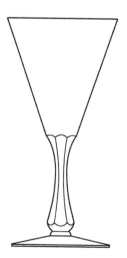

Perfection
Cut 43
Stem 641

Princess
Cut 1120
641

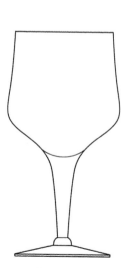

Stem 700

48

Reflection
Stem 708

Cut 1202
708

Cut 1204
708

Feather
*Cut
708*

Holiday
*Cut 1201
708*

708-1
*Cut
708*

Other Stem 708 Patterns:
Cut 1205

Stem 748

Cut 754
748

Cut 756
748

Gourmet
Stem 857
Crystal, or Charcoal Bowl/Crystal Trim

Grecian Pine
*Cut 1221
857*

Symphony
*Cut 1341
857*

Stem 900 Patterns:
"Crackle Barrel"
　　　(Undecorated)

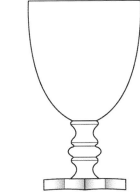

Stem 903
Square Base

49

Cut 228
903

Canterbury
Cut 338
903

Cut 342
903

Laurel
Cut 121
903

Naomi
Blue Bowl/Platinum Encr.
903

903-1
Cut
903

903-2
Cut
903

Other Stem 903 Patterns:
Cut 377

Stem 905

Cut 121
905

Cut 338
905

Cut 480
905

Cut 532
905

Cut 533
905

Cut 781
905

Cut 783
905

905-1
Cut
905

905-2
Cut
905

905-3
Cut
905

Other Stem 905 Patterns:
Cut 433
Cut 490
Cut 496
Cut 516
Cut 688

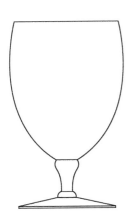

Stem 905 1/2
Available in Crystal or
Moss Green

Cut 1295
905 1/2

Stem 906 Patterns:
Cut 866

Stem 907

Cut "D"
907

Cut 853
907

Cut 923
907

Cut 968
907

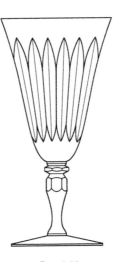

Cut 968
Cut Stem
907

907-1
Cut
907

907-2
*Cut
907*

907-3
*Cut
907*

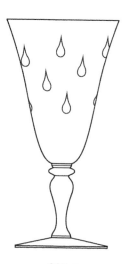

907-4
*Cut
907*

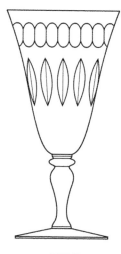

907-5
*Cut
907*

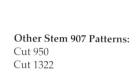

Other Stem 907 Patterns:
Cut 950
Cut 1322
Cut 1323
Cut 1324
Cut 1327   "Enchantment"
Cut 1328

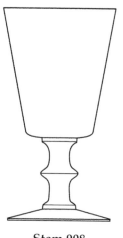

Stem 908

Colonial
*Cut 902
908*

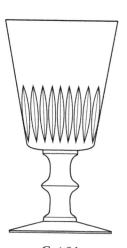

Cut 94
908

Cut 878
908

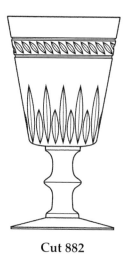

Cut 882
908

Cut 883
908

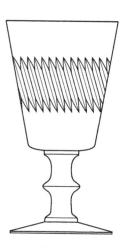

Cut 891
908

Cut 964
908

Cut 974
908

Cut 989
908

Cut 1290
908

Pineapple
Cut
908

Priscilla
Cut
908

Renaissance
Cut 859
908

Tudor
Cut 1294
908

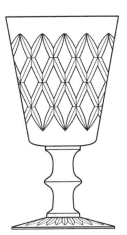

Waterford
Cut 879
908

908-1
Cut
908

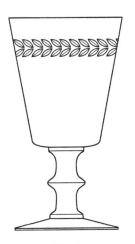

908-2
Cut
908

908-3
Cut
908

908-4
Cut
908

908-5
Cut
908

908-6
Cut
908

Other Stem 908 Patterns:
Cut 654 1/2
Cut 868a   "Pinehurst"
Cut 889
Cut 899
Cut 1160
Cut 1175   "Concord"
Cut 1329

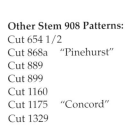

Stem 909
Square Base

Cut 465
909

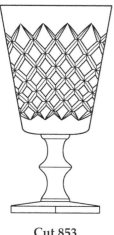

Cut 853
909

Cut 962 1/2
909

Cut 964
909

Cut 970
909

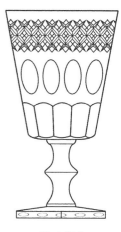

Cut 983
909

Cut 1133
909

Cut 1294
909

Prince of Wales
Cut 859
909

Other Stem 909 Patterns:
Cut 950

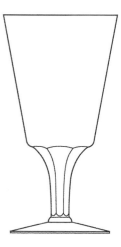

Stem 910

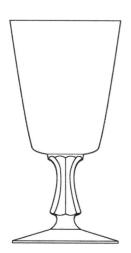

Stem 912

Cut 771
912

Dolly Madison
aka Jane Eyre, Cut 139
912

Edme
Cut 1161
912

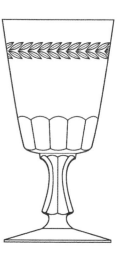

Laurel
Cut 121 & 39
912

Puritan
Cut 1159
912

Ramona
Cut 1006
912

Wickerdale
Cut 1163
912

912-1
Cut
912

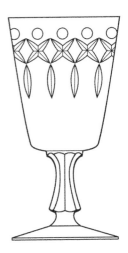

912-2
Cut
912

Other Stem 912 Patterns:
Cut 1005
Cut 1007
Cut 1009
Cut 1105

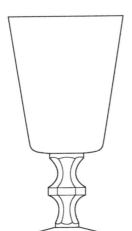

Stem 913

Cut 967
913

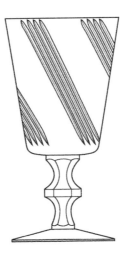

Cut 1028
913

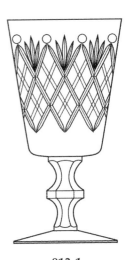

913-1
Cut
913

913-2
Cut
913

Other Stem 913 Patterns:
Cut 1009
Cut 1010

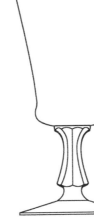

Stem 914

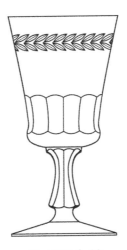

Cut 121 & 39
914

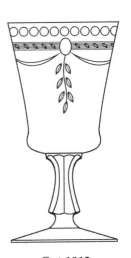

Cut 1012
914

Cut 1013
914

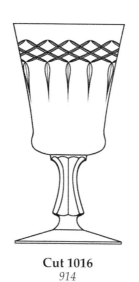

Cut 1015
914

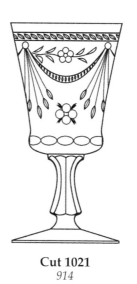

Cut 1016
914

Cut 1021
914

Joyce
Cut
914

Minuet
Cut 1014
914

914-1
Cranberry Flashed
914

Stem 915

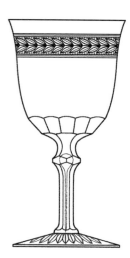

Cut 876
915

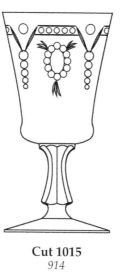

Empire
Cut 918 1/2
915

915-1
Cut
915

915-3
Cut
915

Other Stem 915 Patterns:
Cut 869   "Killarney"
Cut 905   "Carlton"

Stem 916

Cut 870
916

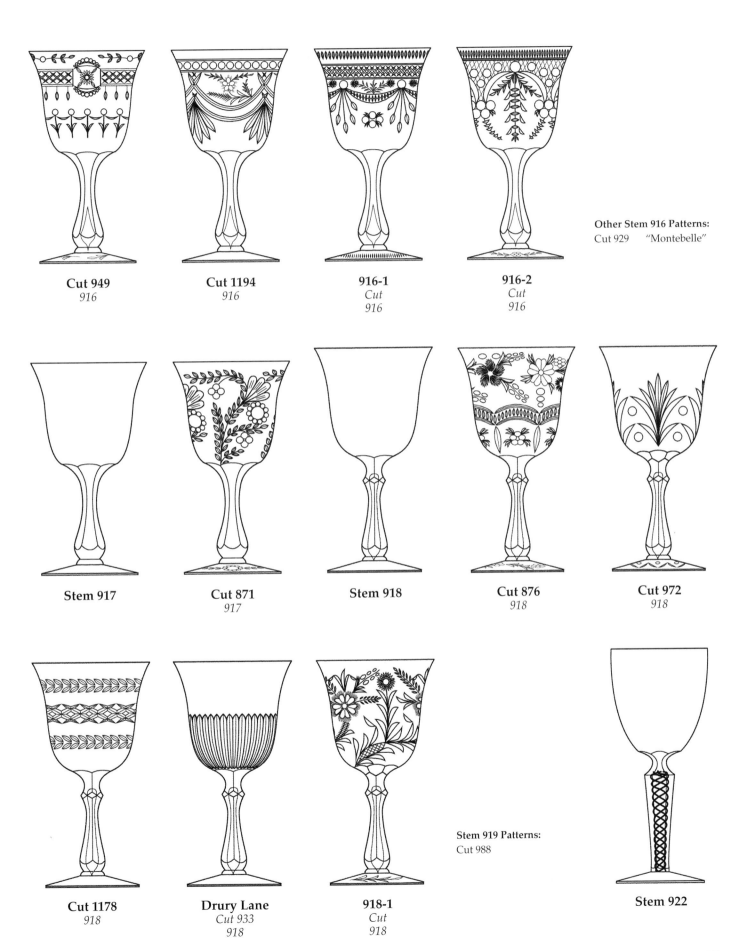

Cut 949
916

Cut 1194
916

916-1
Cut
916

916-2
Cut
916

Other Stem 916 Patterns:
Cut 929   "Montebelle"

Stem 917

Cut 871
917

Stem 918

Cut 876
918

Cut 972
918

Cut 1178
918

Drury Lane
Cut 933
918

918-1
Cut
918

Stem 919 Patterns:
Cut 988

Stem 922

Cut 862
922

Stem 923

Stem 925

Cut 636
925

Cut 880
925

Cut 881
925

925-1
Cut
925

925-2
Cut
925

Other Stem 925 Patterns:
Cut 887
Cut 977

Stem 926

Cut 1075
926

Cut 1130
926

926-1
Cut
926

926-2
Cut
926

Stem 957

Stem 959

Cut 859
959

Cut 879
959

Cut Spikes
959

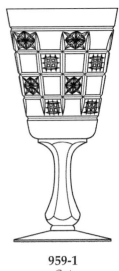

959-1
Cut
959

Stem 960

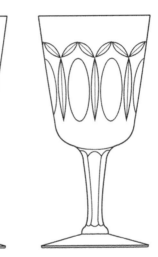

Ardmore
Cut 1436
960

Cambridge
Cut 1433
960

Cut 989
960

Gold Brocade
Cut 1438, Gold Bands
960

Heirloom
Cut 1434
960

Newport
Cut 43
960

Old Master
Cut 1435
960

Radiance
Cut 1437
960

960-1
Cut
960

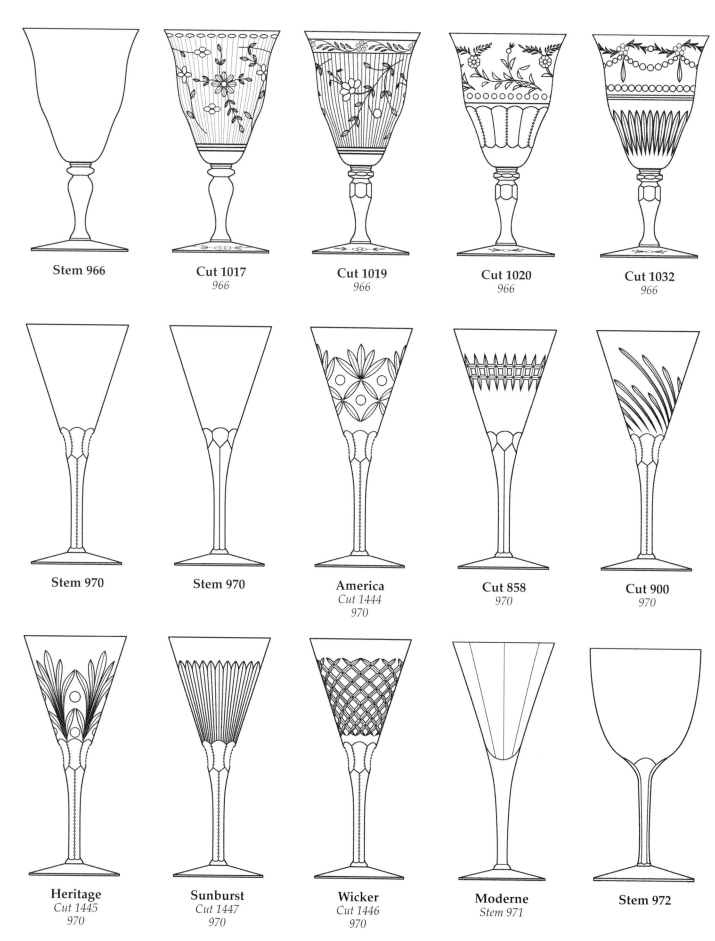

Stem 966

Cut 1017
966

Cut 1019
966

Cut 1020
966

Cut 1032
966

Stem 970

Stem 970

America
Cut 1444
970

Cut 858
970

Cut 900
970

Heritage
Cut 1445
970

Sunburst
Cut 1447
970

Wicker
Cut 1446
970

Moderne
Stem 971

Stem 972

Chalice
Cut 1448
972

Coronet
Cut 1463
972

Garland
Cut 1461
972

Regency
Cut 1462
972

Tapestry
Cut 1449
972

Stem 974

Brittany
Cut 1451
974

Classic
Cut 1450
974

Sculpture
Stem 975

Sculpture was available in Crystal, Delphine Blue, Lime Green, and Sahara.

Reflection
Stem 976

Reflection was available in Brown, Charm Blue, Crystal, Lime, and Yellow.

Fascination
Stem 978

Stem 981

Coronation
Cut 43, Gold Encrusted
981

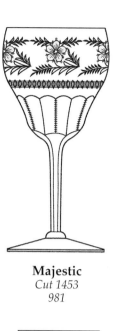

Majestic
Cut 1453
981

Rosalynn
Cut 1452
981

981-1
Cut
981

981-2
Cut
981

Stem 982
Cut 43

Dorchester
Cut 1455
982

Grand Baroque
Cut 1454, aka "Baroque"
982

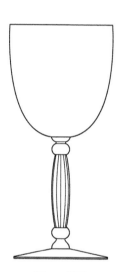

Stem 993

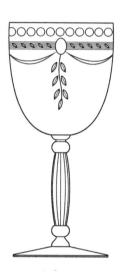

Adams
Cut 1012
993

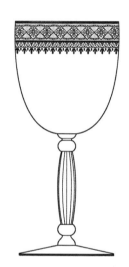

Decoration 551
Gold Encrusted, Gold also
Inside Bowl, 993

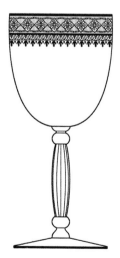

Decoration 552
Gold Encrusted, Gold is
Not Inside Bowl, 993

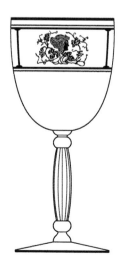

Decoration 553
Gold Inlay, Trim
993

993-1
Cut
993

993-2
Cut
993

993-3
Cut
993

993-4
Cut
993

993-5
Cut
993

Stem 1012

Baubles
Various Colored Stems
Stem 1025

Stem 1030

Stem 1034

Stem 1050

Stem 1050
Black Stem and Foot

Stem 1055

Stem 1060

Stem 1072

Stem 1107

Cut 43
1107

Stem 1108

Stem 1200

Stem 1201

Stem 1202

Cut 76
1202

Cut 101
1202

Cut 159
1202

Cut 220
1202

Cut 360
1202

Engraved 304
1202

Engraved 307
1202

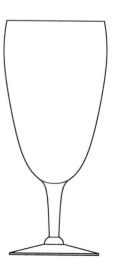

Engraved 320
1202

Engraved 412
1202

NE 12
1202

NE 90
1202

1202-1
Cut
1202

Stem 1203

Stem 1204

Stem 1205

Stem 1207

Stem 1208

Cut 90
1208

NE 15
1208

Stem 1210

Stem 1213

Stem 1214

Stem 1217

Cut 606
1217

Cut 738
1217

Pineapple
Cut 220
1217

1217-1
Cut
1217

Other Stem 1217 Patterns:
Cut 1188

Stem 1219

Stem 1220

Epicure
Stem 1235

The Frank Schoonmaker wine series was made to compliment the Epicure pattern (see page XXIV).

Cut 1419
1235

Juliet
Platinum Trim
1235

Musette
Cut 1406, Platinum Trim
1235

Puritan
Gold Trim
1235

Victoria
Cut 1406, Gold Trim
1235

Windsor
Cut 1406
1235

Stem 1258

1258-1
Cut
1258

1258-2
Cut
1258

1258-3
Cut
1258

Stem 1258 1/2

1258 1/2-1
Cut
1258 1/2

Astrid
Twisted Stem
1282

Hospitality
Cut 43
1282

Buckingham
Cut 1426
1282

Cut 484
1282

Cut 659
1282

Cut 660
1282

Cut 725
1282

Cut 739
1282

Cut 934
1282

Cut 1109
1282

Dayton
Cut 1120
1282

1282-1
Cut
1282

1282-2
Cut
1282

1282-3
Cut
1282

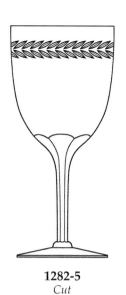

1282-4
Cut
1282

1282-5
Cut
1282

Other Stem 1282 Patterns:
Cut 751

Stem 1293

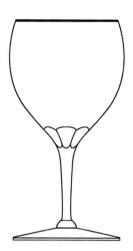

Platinum Crystal Line #5
Platinum Bands
1293

Stem 1350

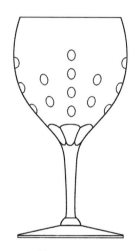

Champagne
Cut 1402
1350

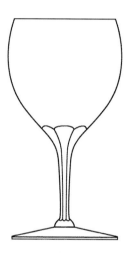

Embassy
Cut 43
1350

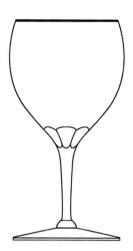

Mansfield
Cut 63, Gold Trim
1350

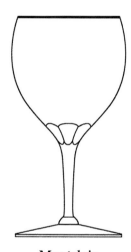

Montclair
Cut 63, Platinum Trim
1350

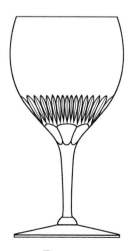

Regency
Cut 1403
1350

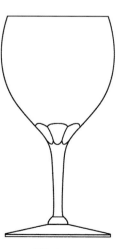

Riviera
Cut 63
1350

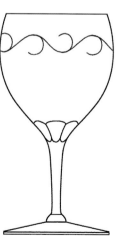

Serenade
Cut 1405
1350

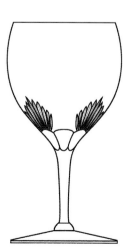

Sunrise
Cut 1404
1350

Weatherly
Cut 1411
1350

1350-1
Cut
1350

1350-2
Cut
1350

1350-3
Cut
1350

1350-4
Cut
1350

1350-5
Cut
1350

1350-6
Cut
1350

1350-7
Cut
1350

Stem 1400

Stem 1476

Cut 627
1476

Stem 1479

Cut 94
1479

Cut 792
1479

Cut 808
1479

Cut 809
1479

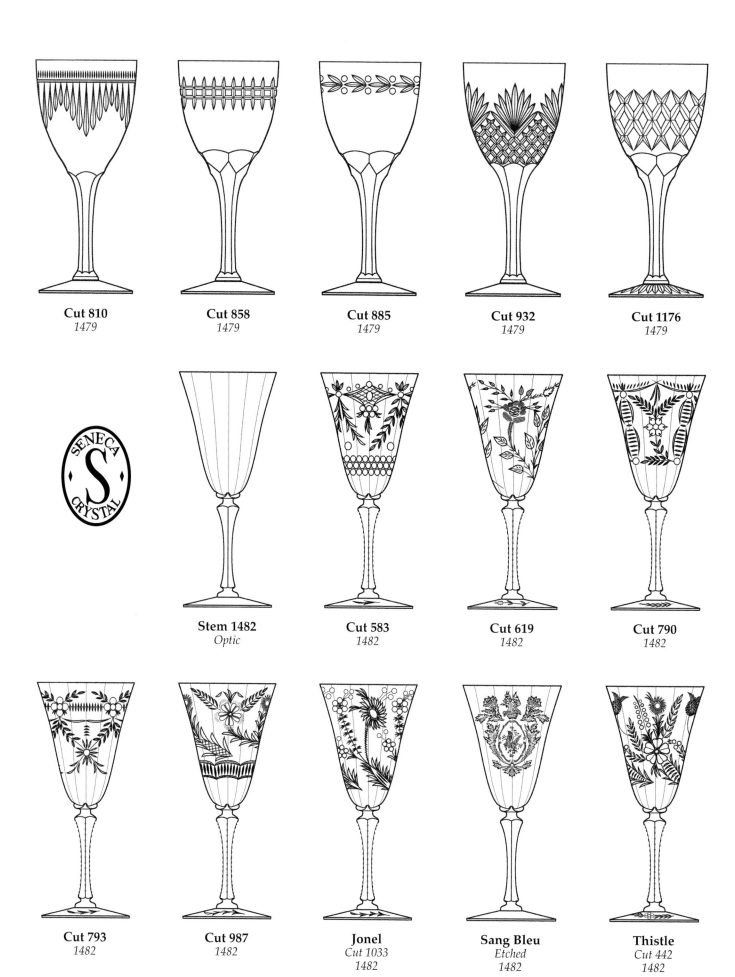

Cut 810
1479

Cut 858
1479

Cut 885
1479

Cut 932
1479

Cut 1176
1479

Stem 1482
Optic

Cut 583
1482

Cut 619
1482

Cut 790
1482

Cut 793
1482

Cut 987
1482

Jonel
Cut 1033
1482

Sang Bleu
Etched
1482

Thistle
Cut 442
1482

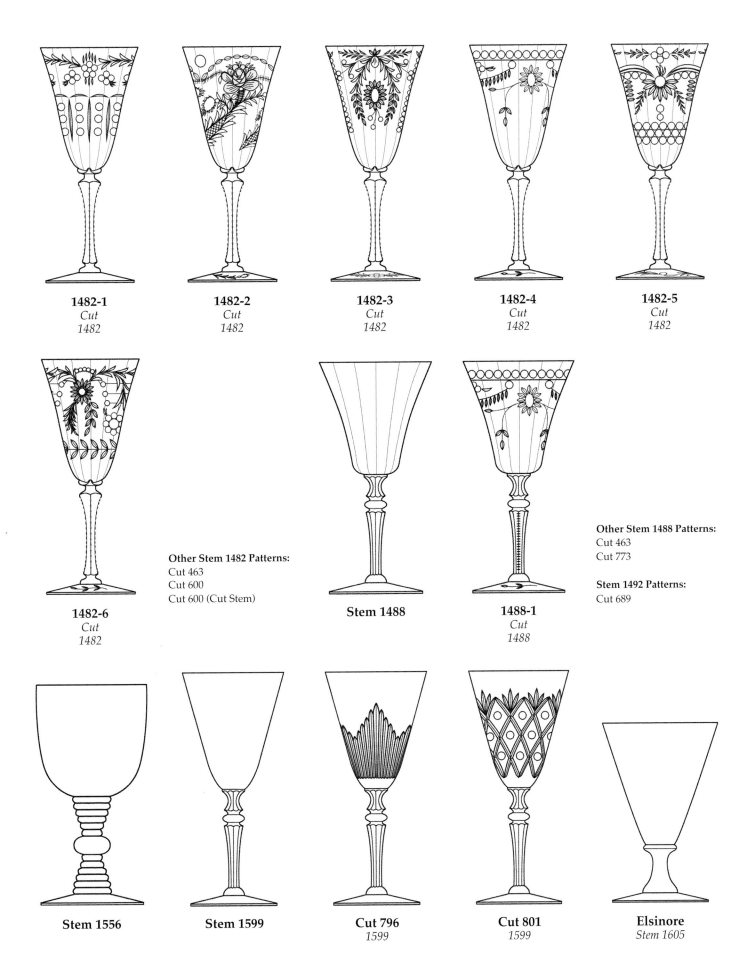

1482-1
Cut
1482

1482-2
Cut
1482

1482-3
Cut
1482

1482-4
Cut
1482

1482-5
Cut
1482

1482-6
Cut
1482

Other Stem 1482 Patterns:
Cut 463
Cut 600
Cut 600 (Cut Stem)

Stem 1488

1488-1
Cut
1488

Other Stem 1488 Patterns:
Cut 463
Cut 773

Stem 1492 Patterns:
Cut 689

Stem 1556

Stem 1599

Cut 796
1599

Cut 801
1599

Elsinore
Stem 1605

Stem 1605 was made available with Gold or Platinum bands, but were not named patterns.

Charcoal
Smoke Bowl
1605

Starburst
Cut 1315
1605

1605-1
Cut
1605

Other Stem 1605 Patterns:
Cut 1312   "Blue Grass"
Cut 1313   "Leaf Dance"
Cut 1314   "Nocturne"

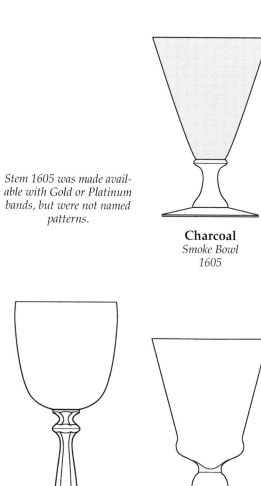

Stem 1693

Stem 1726

Stem 1780

Crinkle Glass
Stem 1820

Crinkle Glass was made available in Accent Red, Crystal, Delphine Blue, Lime Green, Moss Green, and Topaz.

Stem 1892

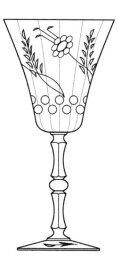

Cut 1066
1892

Stem 1933

1933-1
Cut
1933

1933-2
Cut
1933

Other Stem 1933 Patterns:
Cut 567
Cut 599

Stem 1934

Windsor
Cut 777
1934

1934-1
Cut
1934

Stem 1936

Cut 779
1936

Cut 800
1936

Cut 857
1936

1936-1
Cut
1936

1936-2
Cut
1936

Other Stem 1936 Patterns:
Cut 844   "Chalice"
Cut 856 1/2

Stem 1937
Cut 43

Cut 794
1937

Cut 939
1937

Stem 1938
Cut 43

Cut 795
1938

Stem 1939

Cut 777
1939

Cut 798
1939

1939-1
Cut
1939

1939-2
Cut
1939

Other Stem 1939 Patterns:
Cut 844   "York"
Cut 905   "Victorian"

Stem 1940

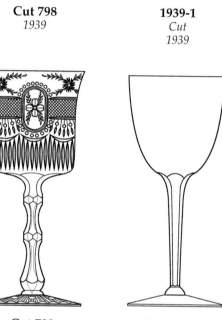

Cut 799
1940

Stem 1941

Cut 800
1941

1941-1
Cut
1941

Other Stem 1941 Patterns:
Cut 800 1/2

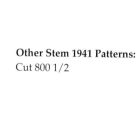

Stem 1951

1951-1
Cut
1951

Stem 1952

1952-1
Cut
1952

1952-2
Cut
1952

Other Stem 1952 Patterns:
Cut 1233   "Hollywreath"
Cut 1243   "Montrose"

Continental
Stem 1962

Chantilly
Gold Trim
1962

Olympia
Platinum Trim
1962

Century
Stem 1963

Arbor
Cut 1460
1963

Bouquet
Cut 1458
1963

Darlene
Cut 1406, Gold Trim
1963

Diane
Cut 1406
1963

Fantasy
Cut 1406, Platinum Trim
1963

First Lady
Cut 1408
1963

Grace
Cut 63
1963

Harvest
Cut 1459
1963

Pristine
Platinum Trim
1963

Sylvia
Gold Trim
1963

True Love
Cut 1409
1963

1963-1
Cut
1963

1963-2
Cut
1963

1963-3
Cut
1963

1963-4
Cut
1963

1963-5
Cut
1963

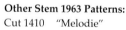

Other Stem 1963 Patterns:
Cut 1410   "Melodie"

Cabaret
Stem 1964

*Cabaret was made available
in Brown/Crystal Foot,
Crystal, Delphine
Blue/Crystal Foot,
Green/Crystal Foot,
Gray/Crystal Foot, and
Yellow/Crystal Foot.*

Andover
Gold Trim
1964

Blue Mist
Blue/Crystal Foot
Platinum, 1964

Carousel
Cut 1412
1964

Copenhagen
Cut 1414
1964

Desert Gold
Brown/Crystal Foot, Gold
1964

Empress
Cut 1424
1964

Greenbrier
Green/Crystal Foot
Platinum, 1964

Lexington
Platinum Trim
1964

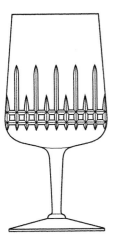

Monte Carlo
Cut 1413
1964

Silver Dawn
Gray/Crystal Foot
Platinum, 1964

Sunset Gold
Yellow/Crystal Foot
Gold, 1964

Whitebrook
Cut 1425
1964

1964-1
Cut
1964

Other Stem 1964 Patterns:
Cut 1415 "Cretan"

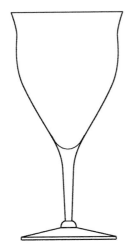

Stem 1965

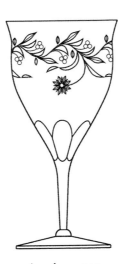

Anniversary
Cut 1421
1965

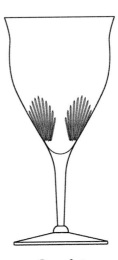

Camelot
Cut 1417
1965

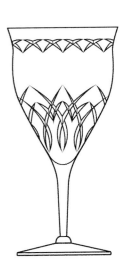

Capistrano
Cut 1423
1965

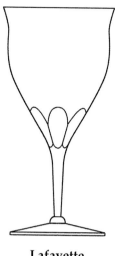

Lafayette
Cut 1416
1965

Orleans
Cut 1422
1965

Princess Anne
Cut 1420
1965

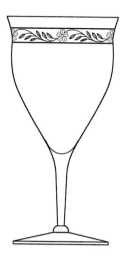

Solitaire
Cut 1419
1965

Tuxedo
Cut 1418
1965

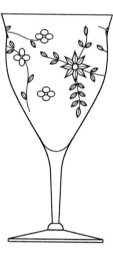

1965-1
Cut
1965

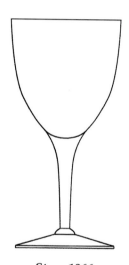

Stem 1966

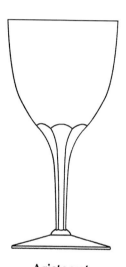

Aristocrat
Cut 43
1966

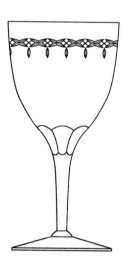

Bridal Tiara
Cut 1439
1966

Cut "A"
(Revised)
1966

Cut 1076
1966

Cut 1114
1966

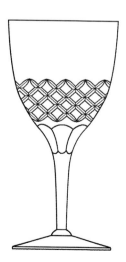

Kimberly
Cut 1430
1966

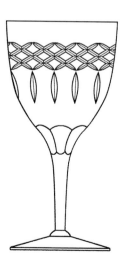

Lavalier
Cut 1431
1966

Traditional
Cut 1432
1966

1966-1
Cut, Gold Trim
1966

1966-2
Cut
1966

1966-3
Cut
1966

1966-4
Cut
1966

Stem 1967

Berkshire
Cut 1427
1967

Chapel Belle
Cut 1440
1967

Sherwood
Cut 1428
1967

Young Love
Cut 1429
1967

1967-1
Cut
1967

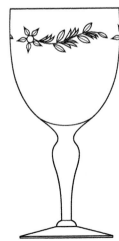

1967-2
Cut
1967

Bouquet
Stem 1969

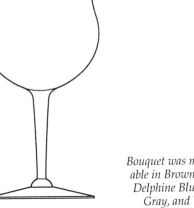

Bouquet was made available in Brown, Crystal, Delphine Blue, Green, Gray, and Yellow.

Debonair
Platinum Band
1969

Grandeur
Gold Band
1969

Reflection
Gold Band on Rim/Foot
1969

Sterling Mist
Sterling Silver Band
1969

Brocado
Stem 1970

Brocado was made available in Avacado (Green), Cristalino (Crystal), Morocco (Brown), Sahara (Yellow), and Toledo (Gray).

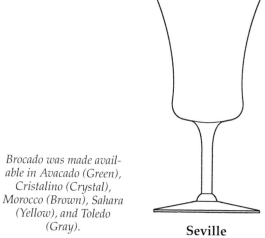

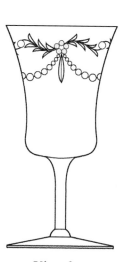

Seville
Stem 1971

Seville was made available in Brown, Crystal, Delphine Blue, Green, Gray, and Yellow.

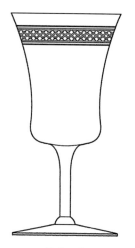

Bristol
Cut 1441, Gold Bands
1971

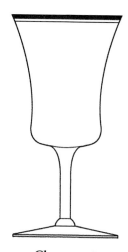

Claremont
Platinum Bands
1971

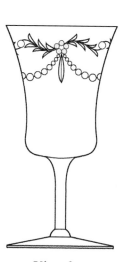

Kingsley
Cut 1442
1971

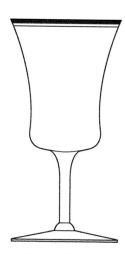

Remembrance
Gold Bands
1971

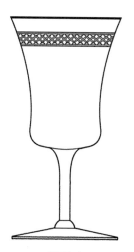

1971-1
Gold Trim
1971

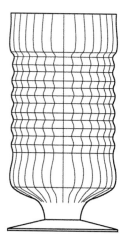

Cascade
Stem 1972

Cascade was made available in Accent Red, Brown, Charm Blue, Crystal, Gray, Lime Green, Moss Green, Peacock Blue, Ritz Blue, and Yellow.

Galaxy
Stem 1973
Clear, Blue, or Pink

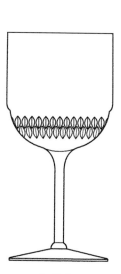

Artistry
Cut 1443
1973

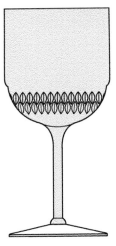

Enchantment
*Cut 1443, Pink/Crystal
Foot, 1973*

Gold Florentine
*Black Decal/Gold Trim
1973*

Intrigue
*Cut 1443, Blue/Crystal
Foot, 1973*

Platinum Lace
*White Decal/Plat. Trim
1973*

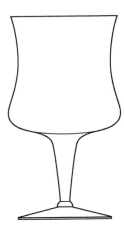

Fashionables
Stem 1974

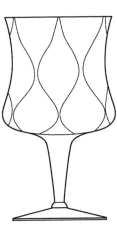

Fashionables
*Hourglass Optic
1974*

*Fashionables was made
available in Accent Red,
Black, Brown, Crystal,
Crystal/Black Foot,
Delphine Blue, Moss
Green, Plum, Ritz Blue,
and Yellow.*

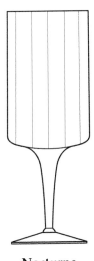

Nocturne
*Stem 1975
Optic*

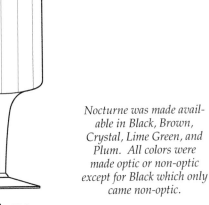

*Nocturne was made avail-
able in Black, Brown,
Crystal, Lime Green, and
Plum. All colors were
made optic or non-optic
except for Black which only
came non-optic.*

Nocturne
*Black, Non-Optic
1975*

Today
Stem 1976

*Today was made available
in Black, Crystal, and
Crystal/Black Foot.*

Le Chateau Series
Stem 1977

Falerno
*Cut 43
1977*

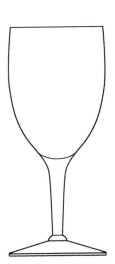

Stem 1978

81

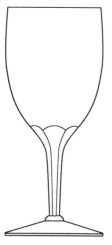

Ultra
Cut 43
1978

Driftwood Casual
Stem 1980

Driftwood Casual was made available in Accent Red, Amber, Amethyst, Amethyst Smoke, Buttercup (Yellow), Charcoal, Charm Blue, Cinnamon (Brown), Crystal, Delphine Blue, Gray, Heather (Pink), Honey, Lime Green, Moss Green, Ocean Blue, Peacock Blue, and Ritz Blue.

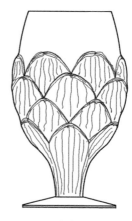

Artichoke
Stem 1985

Artichoke was made available in Accent Red, Brown, Charm Blue, Crystal, Crystal/Black Foot, Delphine Blue, Moss Green, and Yellow.

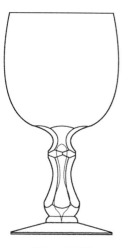

Stem 2000

Cut 941
2000

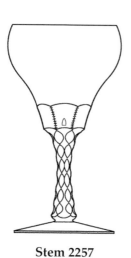

Stem 2257

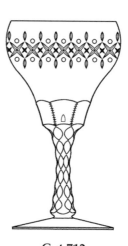

Cut 712
2257

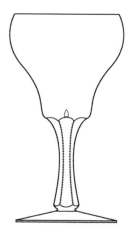

Stem 2258

Cut 709
2258

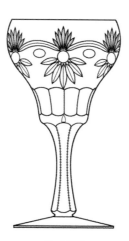

Cut 710
2258

Stem 2493

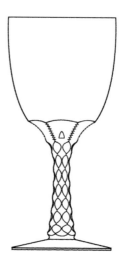

Stem 2502

Cut 716
2502

2502-1
Cut
2502

Stem 2503

Cut 713
2503

Cut 714
2503

Stem 2672

Stem 2690

Stem 2812

Baroque
Cut 1216
2812

Cut 1207
2812

Cut 1209
2812

Cut 1217
2812

Cut 1275
2812

Other Stem 2812 Patterns:
Cut 1225

Stem 3000
Twisted Stem

Stem 3050

Stem 3050
Cut Stem

Cut 936
3050

Decoration 516
Blue Flashed
3050

Harmony
Cranberry Flashed
3050

Starlight
Cut 935
3050

3050-1
Cut
3050

Other Stem 3050 Patterns:
Cut 1106
Cut 1113

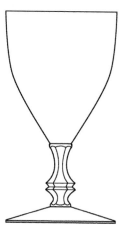

Stem 3214

Stem 3214 was made available with Gold or Platinum bands, but were not named patterns.

Cut 1249
3214

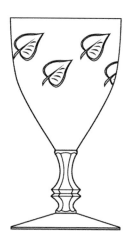

Cut 1250
3214

Cut 1307
3214

Lyric
Cut 1306
3214

Minton
Cut 1303
3214

Morning Star
Cut 1305
3214

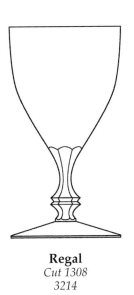

Regal
Cut 1308
3214

Scroll
Cut 1309
3214

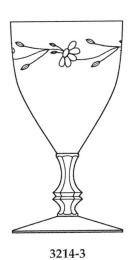

3214-3
Cut
3214

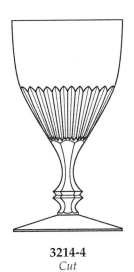

3214-4
Cut
3214

Other Stem 3214 Patterns:
Cut 1304   "Noel"
Cut 1321
Cut 1322
Cut 1382   "Dawn"

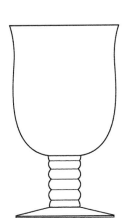

Stem 3600
Clear, Black, or Amber
Foot

Bridal Bouquet
Etched
3600

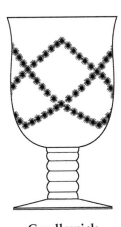

Candlewick
Etched
3600

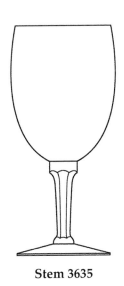

Stem 3635

Other Stem 3635 Patterns:
Cut 1213 1/2 "Accent"
Cut 1269 1/2 "Aristo"
Cut 1366   "Summer Song"

Stem 3691

Stem 3750

Sociables
Line 3875, Crystal, Delphine Blue,
Moss Green, Gray, Plum

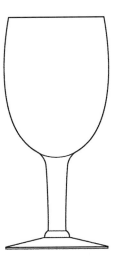

Stem 4000

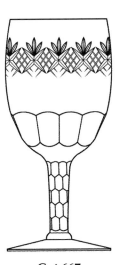

Cut 667
4000

85

Stem 4001

Stem 4805

Berkeley
Cut 779
4805

Cut 800
4805

Cut 907
4805

4805-1
4805

4805-2
4805

Other Stem 4805 Patterns:
Cut 800 1/2
Cut 856 1/2
Cut 956

Stem 4816

Cut 777
4816

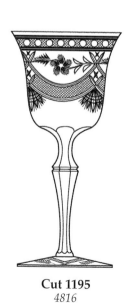

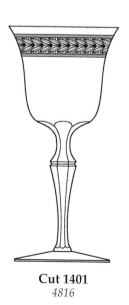

Cut 1195
4816

Cut 1401
4816

4816-1
Cut
4816

4816-2
Cut
4816

Other Stem 4816 Patterns:
Cut 1132   "Sans Souci"
Cut 1196

Stem 4833

Louise
Cut 777
4833

4833-1
Cut
4833

Stem 4850

Stem 4899

Cut 789
4899

Cut 791
4899

Cut 1065
4899

Stem 4993

Stem 5000

Stem 5108

Gourmet Collection
Stem 5321

Chalet
Pink/Crystal Foot
5321

Classic
Cut 1443, Blue/Crystal
Foot, 5321

Connoisseur Collection
Cut 43
5321

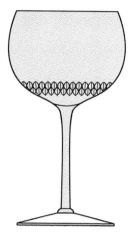

Illusion
*Cut 1443, Pink/Crystal
Foot, 5321*

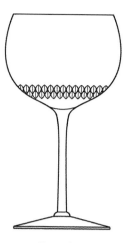

Royalty
*Cut 1443
5321*

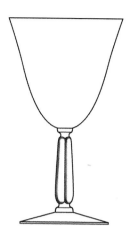

Stem 5325

Belnor
*Teal Blue Bowl, 5325
Also known as "Peacock"*

Silver Swirl
*Cut 1351
5325*

Springtime
*Cut 1399
5325*

Other Stem 5325 Patterns:
Cut 1366   "Cara
Cut 1400   "September
            Serenade"

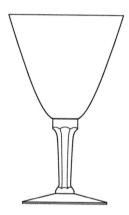

Stem 5335

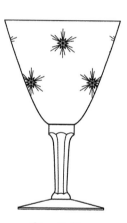

Star Brite
*Cut 1318
5335*

Whirlwind
*Cut 1351
5335*

Other Stem 5335 Patterns:
Cut 1363 1/2
Cut 1400   "Julia"

Stem 5510 Patterns:
Cut 1316
Cut 1317
Cut 1320

Stem 5584

Cut 834
5584

Cut 1063
5584

Stem 6000

Stem 6012

Stem 7000

Stem 7003

Stem 7004

Stem 7490

Stem 8000

Helga
Twisted Stem
Stem 8000

Laurel Wreath
Cut 121
8000

Rose
Etch 609
8000

Scroll
Etch 600
8000

Stem 8833

8833-1
Cut
8833

8833-2
Cut
8833

8833-3
Cut
8833

8833-4
Cut and Etched
8833

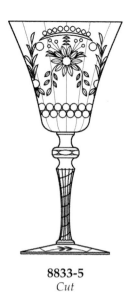

8833-5
Cut 8833

Stem 9078 Patterns:
Cut 784

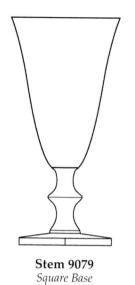

Stem 9079
Square Base

Other Stem 9079 Patterns:
Cut 982

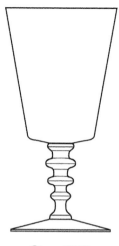

Stem 9088

Cut 975
9088

Stem 9593

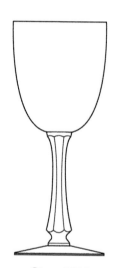

Stem 9936

Colfax
Cut 1002
9936

Cut 739
9936

Cut 991
9936

Cut 992
9936

Cut 1126
9936

Decoration 453
Gold Encrusted
9936

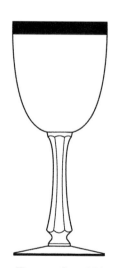

Decoration 461
Gold Band
9936

9936-1
Sterling Encrusted
9936

9936-2
Cut
9936

9936-3
Cut
9936

9936-4
Cut
9936

Other Stem 9936 Patterns:
Cut 739 1/2
Cut 986

Stem 9951

Stardust
Cut 1215
9951

Stem 9972

Stem 9972
Optic

Cut 591
9972

9972-1
Cut
9972

9972-2
Cut
9972

9972-3
Cut
9972

9972-4
Cut
9972

Other Stem 9972 Patterns:
Cut 622
Cut 624

Patterns on
Unknown Stem #'s

Images was made available in Brown, Charm Blue, Crystal, Lime Green, Moss Green, and Yellow.

Images
Stem 10001*

Independence
Various Colors, 10002*
Became part of Images Line

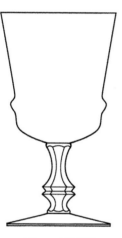

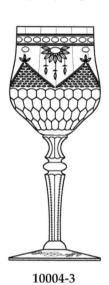

Stem 10003*

Stem 10004*

10004-1
Cut
10004*

10004-2
Cut
10004*

10004-3
Cut
10004*

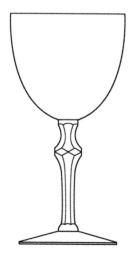

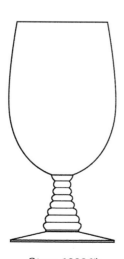

Stem 10005*

Stem 10006*
Seven Ring Stem

Stem 10007*

10007-1
Cut
10007*

Stem 10008*

*Stem numbers 10001 through 10013 are not Seneca factory assigned numbers,
but were assigned by the authors for reference purposes.

Stem 10009*

Stem 10010*

Cut 218
*10010**

Stem 10011*

10011-1
Cut
*10011**

10011-2
Cut
*10011**

Stem 10012*

10012-1
Cut
*10012**

10012-2
Cut
*10012**

Stem 10013*

10013-1
Cut
*10013**

BARWARE

*Patterns with a ** were made in the following colors: Crystal, Delphine Blue, Moss Green, Gray, Plum*

Antique Optic
*3875***

Bellaire
1974

Dundee
1235

Stem numbers 10001 through 10013 are not Seneca factory assigned numbers, but were assigned by the authors for reference purposes.

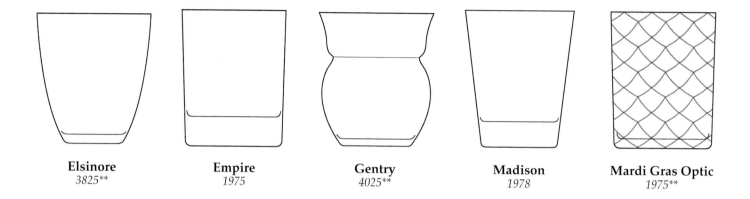

Elsinore
*3825***

Empire
1975

Gentry
*4025***

Madison
1978

Mardi Gras Optic
*1975***

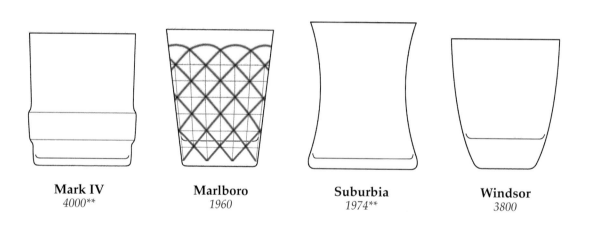

Mark IV
*4000***

Marlboro
1960

Suburbia
*1974***

Windsor
3800

Definitions:
DE - Deep Plate Etching
NE - Needle Etched
NEGD - Needle Etched Gold Decoration

PATTERN INDEX

Note: Patterns which are written in *italics* are from the various pattern matching lists of Seneca. These are patterns which we do not currently have a picture of. They are listed only as a point of reference.

Pattern	Stem/Decoration	Page	Pattern	Stem/Decoration	Page	Pattern	Stem/Decoration	Page
Accent	*3635, C1213 1/2*	*85*	Charcoal	526	46	Cut 273	260	26
Adams	993, C1012	62	Charcoal	1605	72	Cut 286	492	40
Allure	*355, C1363*	*30*	Charcoal Band	526, Platinum	46	Cut 287	492	40
America	970, C1444	60	Claremont	1971, Platinum	80	Cut 293	492	41
Andover	1964, Gold	76	Classic	164, C1121	20	Cut 299	492	41
Anniversary	1965, C1421	77	Classic	974, C1450	61	Cut 300	492	41
Antique Optic	3875	93	Classic	5321, C1443	87	*Cut 326*	*492*	*41*
Arbor	1963, C1460	75	Colfax	9936, C1002	90	*Cut 326*	*515*	*44*
Arcadia	307, C1213	27	Colonial	908, C902	52	Cut 327	492	41
Ardis	352, C1262	28	*Concerto*	*355, C1358*	*30*	Cut 327	515	43
Ardmore	960, C1436	59	*Concord*	*908, C1175*	*53*	Cut 338	905	50
Aristo	*3635, C1269 1/2*	*85*	Connoisseur	405	32	Cut 342	903	50
Aristocrat	1966, C43	78	Connoisseur Collection	5321, C43	87	Cut 358	258	25
Artichoke	1985	82	Continental	1962	75	*Cut 360*	*301*	*27*
Artistry	1973, C1443	80	Copenhagen	1964, C1414	77	Cut 360	1202	64
Asteric	*578, C1377*	*48*	Corinthian	331, C1300	28	Cut 367	499	42
Astral	553, C1362	47	Coronation	352, C1254	28	Cut 369	484	39
Astrid	1282	67	Coronation	981, C43	61	Cut 370	481	37
Avena	578, C1372	48	*Coronet*	*331, C1272*	*28*	Cut 370	515	43
Ballet	405, C1049	32	Coronet	972, C1463	61	Cut 371	499	42
Bancroft	*307, C1335*	*28*	*Corsage*	*578, C1364*	*48*	Cut 372	499	42
Baronet	355, C1334	29	Cosmopolitan	360, C43	30	Cut 373	499	42
Baroque	2812, C1216	83	Countess	515, C638	43	Cut 374	515	43
Baroque	See 'Grand Baroque'	62	Coventry	355, C1325	29	*Cut 377*	*903*	*50*
Baubles	1025	63	*Crackle Barrel*	*900*	*49*	*Cut 405*	*488*	*40*
Bedford	26, C1115	13	*Cretan*	*1964, C1415*	*77*	Cut 414	488	40
Bellaire	355, C1319	29	Crinkle Glass	1820	72	Cut 428	180	21
Bellaire	1974	93	Cut "A"	1966	78	*Cut 432*	*170*	*21*
Belnor	5325	88	Cut "D"	907	51	Cut 432 1/2	170	20
Berkeley	4805, C779	86	Cut "J"	352	29	*Cut 433*	*905*	*51*
Berkshire	1967, C1427	79	Cut 31	475	33	*Cut 437*	*180*	*22*
Bernadette	56, C1355	16	Cut 33	465	33	*Cut 437 1/2*	*180*	*22*
Billingsley Rose	532, C1386	46	Cut 35	150	19	Cut 441	475	33
Blue Grass	*1605, C1312*	*72*	Cut 43	34	14	Cut 453	190	22
Blue Mist	1964, Platinum	76	Cut 43	1107	63	Cut 460	100	18
Blue Ridge	520, C1158	45	Cut 44B	260B	26	Cut 462	100	18
Bouquet	1963, C1458	75	Cut 57	482	38	*Cut 463*	*1482*	*71*
Bouquet	1969	79	Cut 58	482	38	*Cut 463*	*1488*	*71*
Bradford	128, C1276	18	Cut 61	482	38	Cut 465	909	53
Bridal Bouquet	3600	85	Cut 62	486	40	Cut 468	100	18
Bridal Tiara	1966, C1439	78	Cut 64	482	38	*Cut 471*	*190*	*24*
Brilliant	*164, C1031*	*20*	Cut 64	485	39	Cut 480	905	50
Bristol	1971, C1441	80	Cut 76	1202	64	*Cut 481*	*190*	*24*
Brittany	974, C1451	61	Cut 90	1208	65	Cut 484	1282	67
Brocado	1970	80	Cut 94	476	34	*Cut 490*	*905*	*51*
Buckingham	1282, C1426	67	Cut 94	908	52	Cut 498	190	22
Buttercup	517, C1162	44	Cut 94	1479	69	*Cut 496*	*905*	*51*
Butterfly	475, C786	33	Cut 94	1202	64	*Cut 516*	*905*	*51*
Cabaret	1964	76	Cut 101	100	18	Cut 532	905	50
Cambridge	960, C1433	59	Cut 121 & 39	914	55	Cut 533	905	50
Camelot	1965, C1417	77	Cut 121	164	20	*Cut 536*	*190*	*24*
Candlewick	3600	85	*Cut 121*	*517*	*44*	Cut 560	34	14
Canterbury	903, C338	50	Cut 121	520	45	Cut 561	100	18
Capistrano	405	32	Cut 121	905	50	*Cut 567*	*1933*	*73*
Capistrano	1965, C1423	77	Cut 159	1202	64	Cut 583	1482	70
Caprice	352, C1229	28	Cut 204	459	33	Cut 591	9972	91
Cara	*5325, C1366*	*88*	Cut 218	482	38	*Cut 593*	*476*	*37*
Carlton	*915, C905*	*56*	Cut 218	10010	93	*Cut 594*	*484*	*39*
Carousel	1964, C1412	76	Cut 219	477	37	*Cut 596*	*180*	*22*
Cascade	1972	80	Cut 220	1202	64	Cut 597	180	21
Celeste	355, C1318	29	Cut 221	477	37	*Cut 599*	*1933*	*73*
Century	1963	75	Cut 228	903	50	*Cut 600*	*1482*	*71*
Chalet	5321	87	Cut 250	150	19	*Cut 600*	*1482 (Cut Stem)*	*71*
Chalice	972, C1448	61	Cut 258	475	33	*Cut 601*	*180*	*22*
Chalice	*1936, C844*	*73*	Cut 259	482	38	Cut 606	1217	65
Champagne	1350, C1402	68	Cut 260	482	38	Cut 619	1482	70
Chanelle	492, Platinum	40	Cut 261	492	40	Cut 627 1/2	515	43
Chantilly	1962, Gold	75	Cut 262	493	41	Cut 627	1476	69
Chapel Belle	1967, C1440	79	Cut 263	34	14	*Cut 628*	*476*	*37*

97

REPLACEMENTS, LTD.

Replacements, Ltd., the world's largest supplier of obsolete, inactive and active china, crystal, flatware and collectibles, was founded by Bob Page in 1981. The company evolved out of Page's weekend hobby of visiting flea markets for vintage china and crystal. Last year, Replacements recorded $31.5 million in sales - its best sales year ever -and is projecting $40 million in business for 1995. "It's an ever-growing business that never ceases to amaze me," says Page, who worked as an auditor for the state of North Carolina prior to forming Replacements. The company now employs over 300.

A view of the 8,000-square-foot showroom, looking into the museum area.

The firm locates hard-to-find pieces for over 800,000 customers. Customers write or call about their patterns at a rate of 90,000 per month. Many inquiries are from individuals seeking to replace or add pieces to their discontinued table-settings. Others are from persons wishing to sell patterns.

Replacements stocks 3 million pieces of inventory in 58,000 patterns. Designs are from the 19th and 20th century. Replacements relies on a network of 3,000 independent suppliers who shop flea markets, estate sales and auctions for mint condition pieces to sell to Replacements. Also, the company makes bulk purchases of discontinued patterns from manufacturers, including such well-known names as Royal Doulton, Noritake, Mikasa, Lenox, Wedgwood and Haviland China. Page says some manufacturers and retailers have come to regard Replacements not only as a potential customer for old inventory, but as part of their own customer service.

In late '94, the company expanded its warehouse/office facility to 225,000-square-feet, or the size of four football fields. The new building includes an 8,000-square-foot showroom with an adjoining 2,300-square-foot museum. Both areas are filled with antique walnut, oak and mahogany showcases, and feature giftware, antiques, one-of-a-kind items, collectibles and special purchases of tableware.

The Replacements, Ltd. Museum of Tableware and Decorative Arts houses a permanent collection of rare and unusual pieces. There is a special focus on the early 20th century glass industry of the Ohio Valley region, including glassware from Tiffin, Fostoria, Heisey, Cambridge and Imperial.

Replacements, Ltd. offers free public tours of its museum, office and warehouse facility. The unique tours attract about 2,500 visitors a month and have been featured on CNN's Travel Guide and in Southern Living magazine. Tour highlights include a stop at the research department where tour participants see curators busy at work identifying mystery patterns and piece types. Consulting manufacturers' price lists, catalogs, photographs and other valuable reference materials housed in this department helps Replacements identify over 500 patterns every week for its customers, there is no charge for this service.

A walk through the china inventory department provides an opportunity to observe how china is inspected for flaws or defects. Approximately 40,000 pieces of china are evaluated weekly by Replacements' employees. China must be free of cracks or chips to be purchased by the company.

Tour patrons learn how minor knicks are removed from crystal stemware, how worn gold or platinum trim on china is repaired, and how crazed or scratched earthenware is refired in kilns to look like new. Because the restoration process is very delicate it is not offered to the public.

In the flatware department, tour-goers see how sterling, silver plate, and stainless steel items are polished on high-speed buffing machines. They also get to see "Before & After" examples of repair jobs, some damaged from home accidents such as falling in the garbage disposal, etc. Replacements, Ltd. does offer polishing and flatware repair services to the public.

Shown is a Noritake dinner plate being regilded. The heat in one of the company's eight kilns will permanently bond the gold to the plate – restoring the trim to its original condition.

Individual tours are scheduled every half hour from 8:30 a.m. EST to 8:30 p.m. daily. Group tours of 20 or more should be arranged in advance and tour bus parking is available.

Replacements, Ltd. recently began putting together a series of pattern identification guides on china, crystal and flatware, including this book on Seneca. To help create the books, employees scan printed images of patterns into a computer system to produce sharp, unmistakable line drawings of the designs.

Other books on various glass manufacturers in addition to identification guides on china are in the future plans of Replacements, Ltd.

For additional information, call toll free:1-800-562-4462 or fax us at 1-910-697-3100. If you would like to write us (we'd love to here from you), our address is: Replacements, Ltd., 1089 Knox Road, P.O. Box 26029, Greensboro, N.C. 27420-6029.

REPLACEMENTS, LTD.
China, Crystal & Flatware

1-800-562-4462

ABOUT THE AUTHORS

Bob Page was born April 19, 1945 and grew up working the fields of his family's small tobacco farm in Ruffin, North Carolina. He attended the University of North Carolina at Chapel Hill and graduated with a degree in business and a major in accounting. After two years in the U.S. Army, he obtained his CPA certificate and worked in public accounting for eight years. In 1978, he took a position as an auditor for the State of North Carolina.

In March of 1981, Bob left his accounting career forever to form Replacements, Ltd. He and his company have received extensive publicity and public recognition. Awards include the North Carolina Excellence Award presented by Governor James Martin, North Carolina Small Businessman of the Year, a ranking of #81 in Inc. magazine's annual list of America's fastest-growing privately-held companies (1986), North Carolina Person of the Week from UNC Center for Public Television and 1991 Retail Entrepreneur of the Year for the State of North Carolina. Page is also involved in a number of charitable endeavors and currently serves on the board of the Triad Health Project (a local AIDS support organization).

Dale Frederiksen was born June 15, 1962 in Pontiac, Michigan and attended Waterford Township High School. In 1980, Frederiksen moved to Chattanooga, Tennessee to attend Tennessee Temple University, graduating in 1984 with a BS degree in secondary education. He taught junior and senior high mathematics for three years in Kansas City, Kansas, returning to Chattanooga in 1987 to teach mathematics and to coach volleyball at Ooltewah Middle School. In 1989, he joined the staff of Replacements, Ltd. as an inventory purchasing agent and later trained in the field of computer graphics, where he has created or supervised the creation of most of the images in this book. Frederiksen enjoys researching and discovering patterns that have previously been undocumented. He also enjoys accompanying his companion, Bob Page, on buying trips around the world. His hobbies include tennis, volleyball and visiting flea markets.

Other Books By Page-Frederiksen Publishing

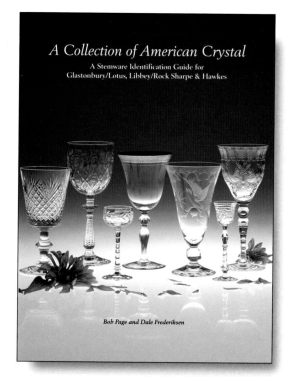

"Tiffin is Forever: A Stemware Identification Guide" (1994) This comprehensive reference guide on Tiffin stemware showcases the wide array of patterns made by Tiffin Glass from the 1920's to the 1980's. This book pictures over 2,700 stems and patterns, some never having been shown together before. This guide is a must for the glass enthusiast or collector. $29.95, add $2.00 for shipping and handling.

"A Collection of American Crystal: A Stemware Identification Guide for Glastonbury/Lotus, Libbey/Rock Sharpe & Hawkes" (1995) An extensive reference guide, designed to document stems and patterns of the Glastonbury and Lotus Glass Companies, the Libbey Glass Company emphasizing the Rock Sharpe division, and the T.G. Hawkes Glass Company. Three manufacturers in one. $24.95, add $2.00 for shipping and handling.

Other Identification Guides From Replacements, Ltd.:

Replacements, Ltd. Crystal Identification Guide - a soft cover identification guide containing pictures of several American and European glass companies including Baccarat, Fostoria, Galway, Mikasa, Waterford and others. Designed to be used in conjunction with the Replacements, Ltd. Suppliers' Index, this guide gives a representation of many glass manufacturers. $15.00, shipping included (in USA).

Replacements, Ltd. Stainless Flatware Identification Guide - a soft cover identification guide containing over 2,000 pictures of stainless steel flatware from over 60 manufacturers. An exhaustive listing from Replacements' extensive literature with backstamp information and descriptions. Intended for use with the Replacements, Ltd. Suppliers' Index. $20.00, shipping included (in USA).

All books are available from:
Replacements, Ltd.
1089 Knox Road, PO Box 26029
Greensboro, NC 27420
1-800-562-4462